Praise for *Brand Singapore*

"Few governments have moulded their country's image as consciously and diligently as Singapore's. Koh Buck Song has written an illuminating and entertaining account of the building of Singapore's 'brand', an effort so successful that its politicians sometimes seem to confuse their country with a Fortune 500 company."

SIMON LONG
The Economist, United Kingdom

"Koh is a writer of style and substance on country branding. His book is a must-read for anyone interested in place branding on a national scale, especially in the Asian region."

PROFESSOR RUTH RENTSCHLER
University of South Australia Business School, Australia

"A must-read for all policy-makers and business leaders, who are struggling to survive in the ever-intensifying global competition. Building the brand of a nation is not magic. There are fine-tuned mechanisms and strong volition behind the front stage. The secret of Singapore's success is precisely uncovered by Koh Buck Song."

YASU OTA
Nikkei Asian Review, Japan

"Koh's well-documented story (on Singapore) offers inspiring ideas… it is almost a declaration of love to place branding by a prominent practitioner in the field."

GRUPO TASO
Place branding consultants, Spain

"Koh provides a highly illuminating account of Singapore's nation branding. The acknowledgement of the political environment within which nation branding occurs is a particularly welcome contribution to the place branding literature."

DR KEITH DINNIE
Nation Branding: Concepts, Issues, Practice (Routledge), UK

"A wonderful way to describe how to create excitement for a country, define its spirit, and sell its promises."

DR RAFARAVAVITAFIKA RASATA
Ministry of Foreign Affairs, Republic of Madagascar

"Beyond telling Singapore's brand story in such a clear and easy-to-read book, Koh has managed to take readers into a journey that conciliates core concepts from the academic shores of place making, place branding and place marketing strategies, with the practitioner's trails."

DANIEL VALVERDE BAGNARELLO
Nation Brand Director, Costa Rica

Brand Singapore

BRAND SINGAPORE

THIRD EDITION

Nation Branding in a World
Disrupted by Covid-19

KOH BUCK SONG

First edition published in 2011; second edition published in 2017

This third edition published in 2021 by Marshall Cavendish Business
An imprint of Marshall Cavendish International

A member of the
Times Publishing Group

Other Marshall Cavendish Offices:
Marshall Cavendish Corporation, 800 Westchester Ave, Suite N-641, Rye Brook, NY 10573, USA • Marshall Cavendish International (Thailand) Co Ltd, 253 Asoke, 16th Floor, Sukhumvit 21 Road, Klongtoey Nua, Wattana, Bangkok 10110, Thailand • Marshall Cavendish (Malaysia) Sdn Bhd, Times Subang, Lot 46, Subang Hi-Tech Industrial Park, Batu Tiga, 40000 Shah Alam, Selangor Darul Ehsan, Malaysia

Marshall Cavendish is a registered trademark of Times Publishing Limited

National Library Board, Singapore Cataloguing in Publication Data

Names: Koh, Buck Song.
Title: Brand Singapore : Nation branding in a world disrupted by Covid-19 / Koh Buck Song.
Description: Third edition. | Singapore : Marshall Cavendish Business, 2021. | Includes index.
Identifiers: OCN 1200192267 | ISBN 978-981-4928-38-0 (paperback)
Subjects: LCSH: Place marketing—Singapore. | National characteristics, Singaporean. | Branding (Marketing)—Singapore.
Classification: DDC 959.5700688—dc23

Printed in Singapore

For Dora,
whose brand of zest for life
enriches Singapore,
even as it extends far beyond

The author would like to express deep appreciation
and gratitude to Keith Dinnie, Florian Kaefer,
Simon Long, Jonathan McClory, Yasu Ota,
Rafaravavitafika Rasata, Ruth Rentschler,
Daniel Valverde Bagnarello, Adithi Khandadi,
Justin Lau and Melvin Neo.

CONTENTS

INTRODUCTION

THE COVID-19 PANDEMIC that surfaced in late 2019 has turned the world upside-down. By the end of August 2020, this coronavirus strand had already claimed more than 24 million known cases, and more than 820,000 deaths worldwide. The global economy, totally upturned, will take years to recover. But the fundamentals of place branding have maintained their centre of gravity. When human wellbeing is being washed aside by relentless tsunamis of asymptomatic infections, and foreign aid, international collaboration and most travel are being kept ashore by waves of protectionism and currents of deglobalisation, anyone venturing out must tread water more carefully, and try to swim towards the dry land of safe, welcoming and trustworthy country brands.

Brand Singapore

Reputation is precious, now more than ever. Of all earthly possessions, your brand is the most valuable thing you could have for moving up in the world – whether as a person, company or country. Without a good CV, you would not be entrusted with a high-level job. For businesses, success rests on corporate standing and customer support, both of which start with having a good name. As for countries, only the most attractive and respected places have the power to draw top talent and hot money. With country brands, larger nations have some room for manoeuvre – they could even take a few knocks and still proceed unscathed. But for small states, a nation brand is all the more valuable because, in some cases, a good reputation is the main asset – perhaps the only one that can be built up with human effort – to attract tourism and other inflows of people, goods and services.[1]

All these realities of country branding and brand-building are being challenged even more today, in the light of global developments since the start of the 2010s, and now, all the more in a world totally disrupted by Covid-19, with the lifeblood of place brand-building – the movement of people and goods, cultural events, enjoyment of food, entertainment and other cultural products – all but halted. Even before the pandemic, the global village was already fragmenting. Countries that used to lead in global rankings of country brands have seen their nation brands damaged, as their politics and societies have become more divided and divisive. The two prime examples of this were both seen to emerge in the same year of 2016, in Britain after the Brexit vote in the June 2016 referendum to leave the European Union, and in the United States after the controversial election of President Donald Trump in November 2016, leading to the whole country being referred to by *Time* magazine as the "divided states of America".[2] Under the administration of President George W. Bush from 2000 to 2008, the USA's divisive effect was external, leaving the world more fractured, mainly because of its hardline Middle East foreign policy. Now, internal forces from within threaten to tear the country itself apart. The first term of the Trump administration saw the USA stumbling to the brink of civil war, exacerbated by the politicisation of public health and the fallout from the rash of Covid-19 cases and deaths, and the Black Lives Matter protests.

Across the world, the socio-political forces of extremism and populism have come to the fore in individual countries in an unprecedented way. At the same time, the accompanying developments of withdrawal from some key aspects of globalisation, including greater protectionism and curbs on trade and immigration – leading to an inevitable drag on individual mobility, tourism and investment – have transformed the global context in which nation brands can assert themselves and compete. Singapore is an open trading nation, with its trade more than three times the size of its gross domestic product, one of the world's highest ratios. A rules-based global trading system, based on respect for the rule of law and international norms, is essential to its growth. Having a strong brand is vital to its relations with trading partners.

In the field of nation branding and brand-building, Singapore continues to be a fascinating case study. By consciously creating and cultivating a country brand, the island – geographically small at just over 720 sq km, but internationally influential beyond its physical size – pulled itself up from next to nothing to become Asia's forerunner in the league of leading nations. For example, in the 2019 ranking of the Country Brand Index, a global survey of 75 countries' reputations by the brand agency FutureBrand, Singapore held its own as a representative of Asia, being ranked 18th overall, second in Asia after Japan (ranked number 1 globally). In the sub-category of most influential cities, Singapore kept its position at 12th place. The republic's relatively high placings are due, in large part, to a unique Singapore-style brand guardianship – unusual in the way the country's brand is shaped for its own people as well as in the way it is displayed to the world. This book assesses this remarkable brand journey, as well as the challenges for the future in a new world order.

Chapter 1 explains the concept of nation branding, and positions Singapore's global standing in this space. Terms like "brand equity" and "brand ambassadors" are described. Following that, the nation branding of Singapore is examined through the three main spheres of society: the public, private and people sectors.

Chapter 2, on the government's "visible hand" in nation branding, considers how the state plays the biggest role, as it does in most other spheres of life in Singapore. This chapter reveals a measure of the extent of central coordination in terms of social, economic and political policy, thereby indirectly building and sustaining Singapore's strongest brand attributes. Of the four sub-brands, the tourism brand journey is the best-known, culminating in the "Passion Made Possible" brand launched in 2017, the most effective concept thus far. Today, these forces are being adjusted, with the passing away in 2015 of Lee Kuan Yew, Singapore's first prime minister, marking a shift into a new era of country brand-building without Mr Lee's direct influence. The introduction of the reserved Presidency, a bold political move, positioned Singapore significantly in terms of global brand awareness of the multiculturalism that the city-state is admired for. The carefully curated Singapore Bicentennial year of 2019 marked another new phase, reaffirming key fundamentals of Singapore's relationship with its colonial past, and opening up a whole new way of looking at the island's 700 years of ancient heritage.

Chapter 3 looks at Singapore's corporate sector, including some key characteristics of how business people and organisations behave in relation to the country brand, as well as how the private sector has produced some global winners, and asks: Can business players do more, and how?

Chapter 4 takes stock of contributions made by individual Singaporeans to the country brand in all forms of creativity, including playing with Singlish, from arts and entertainment to sports and diplomacy, as well as the activities and achievements that have attracted the attention of significant foreign audiences, sometimes without directly meaning to. The game-changing impact of the "SG50" year is examined – a whole year in 2015 of citizen engagement to celebrate Singapore's golden jubilee of independence. For external audiences, the Hollywood movie *Crazy Rich Asians* brought global brand affinity for Singapore to a whole new level, even as it sparked some soul-searching at home about minority representation.

Chapter 5 offers an analysis of the deeper meaning behind Singapore's chief national icons, such as the Merlion, and argues for a more holistic and comprehensive way of thinking about the symbols that influence the country brand.

Chapter 6 follows with a critique of troublesome international perceptions that have stuck, and whether these "brand keloids" – enduring scars on the reputation – pose obstacles to brand-building. The extent of the "stickiness" of these negative perceptions is evaluated, especially the "nanny state" tag. On the socio-political aspect of brand Singapore, the general elections of 2011, 2015 and 2020 are discussed in relation to what they reveal about the nature of governance and of the agency of the electorate, which flesh out realities beyond most external preconceptions.

Chapter 7 assesses the case of the official nation branding project "The Spirit of Singapore" from the 2000s, and contemplates the future of Singapore as a country brand against the backdrop of a world of deglobalisation that is becoming less open and welcoming in terms of trade, tourism, immigration and investment. Singapore's fondness for maritime national metaphors and analogies is also discussed. The impact of the Covid-19 pandemic is explored, including the damage it has already caused, and the direct and indirect effects on the future of Singapore's country branding.

Singapore's traditional plus points of its brand attributes – clustered around efficiency and effectiveness – are well-known to those who admire them. Among this group are many people, whether from developing countries or the most advanced states, who have seen worse in their own backyards and look up to the Lion City. To what extent has nation branding accounted for the republic's dramatic rise in more than five decades, over and above its many other "secrets of success"? And if a good name requires constant, conscious and coordinated cultivation, what are Singapore's chances of continuing to do this, and moving up even higher in the world? Can it succeed in its ambition to be a leading global city? Has the very idea of a global city changed, with new questions being asked about globalisation itself, and now, with all the displacements brought by Covid-19? In the pursuit of progress, development and quality of life, could the method and manner of Singapore's nation branding, in fact, be the most important secret of all?

CHAPTER 1

FOR HEARTS
AND MINDS

Once upon a country brand...

YOU KNOW THE TYPE: ask them to choose between two restaurants for dinner, and they hem and haw, and hem and haw. Their protestations range from the robustly courteous ("I really don't mind; you choose...") to the blatantly false ("I eat everything!"). Finally, you ask: "Okay, what if I were to put a gun to your head for a reply on the count of three, which one would you pick? Don't hesitate, just say the first name that comes to mind." If you're lucky, you finally get an answer. That answer is due to branding.

That final selection draws on what is called, in the vocabulary of branding, "top-of-mind recall". When a subject is mentioned, the first name that comes to mind is the one that has managed to connect and register most readily with the person making a decision. In the corporate branding industry, people are routinely gathered in focus groups and asked questions to test, for example, which brands they mention on the spur of the moment, and also to reveal what they instinctively think and feel about these brands. The brands most often cited without hesitation are those that have secured top place in the short-term memory of their target audiences. This process is called "brand recall" – and the even more valuable type of this data is "unaided brand recall", when respondents are not prompted which option to select (for example, asking "Which restaurant do you think is best for steak?" with no options given). For any brand, attaining a high level of unaided brand recall gives a significant competitive advantage in that particular brand space. If you can get many people to think of your brand first before others, it means that the chances of your brand being picked in a buying decision are that much greater.

The value of branding

Branding, then, is the sum total of actions taken to shape the perception of something, someone or some location, so as to achieve and maintain top-of-mind awareness. It refers to conscious and deliberate efforts to create and cultivate an image for a product, party, person or place. Advertising and public relations are the usual communications approaches employed, through platforms including the mainstream media, online social media and third-party endorsement.

In the branding process, assets and advantages are highlighted, and sometimes grossly exaggerated. At the same time, flaws and faults are set aside or even covered up. Branding can be very loud or very soft. It includes the most public and expensive proclamations, such as billboard ads for luxury consumer products – from limousines to lingerie – across the globe. Or, it can entail zero extra dollar cost, because branding also includes taking basic measures of self-improvement, such as a company getting its customer relations staff to do better based on user feedback and then informing customers about it using existing channels of communication.

A key difference between marketing and branding is that marketing deals with things that are more concrete, whereas branding is more abstract. Marketing usually involves applying hard power facets such as pricing and product quality, or offering discounts or freebies, trying to entice customers with material sweeteners. By contrast, branding is more concerned with promoting brand attributes – characteristics that other people can recognise and appreciate. Branding is about intangibles – for example, the very idea of Singapore – with a soft power approach to win attention and affection for brand awareness and affinity, so that other people know your brand and like it, even if they may never pay any money to buy anything from you. Marketing highlights more superficial qualities, while branding seeks to grasp quintessential character. One way to tell whether an action is more marketing or branding is to see whether it has an easily measured quantitative key performance indicator (KPI) – if it does, it's probably more marketing than branding. Overall, branding is more holistic and comprehensive, and marketing is, in fact, a subset of branding.

And branding is not all about profit and sales. Branding can also be done – indeed, needs to be done – just as much by non-profit organisations. Often, the lack of impact in general of non-profit organisations in advancing their causes can be put down to lack of branding. The more people know of, and think well of, a group – for-profit or non-profit – the more likely they will support the cause it promotes. Some of this branding can be free advertising (at least with no immediate dollar cost) – increasingly an option through "viral marketing" via online social media. Some of it is good public relations, through doing things right and influencing others to recognise it and compliment you for doing it or refer others to you.

Most of the time, branding is an expensive business. Advertising space is costed on perceived value. The process goes like this: Talent is vital to create branding concepts to begin with; man-hours are then essential to execute those plans and make the branding come to life; and, hopefully, the returns should be more than worthwhile. Good branding is worth paying for, if you consider that a reputation is the ultimate intangible asset, whether for one man or woman, or a huge global corporation, or a country or even a whole region. Multinational companies spend millions of dollars to construct and protect their corporate standing. Revenue, profit, growth, their very survival – all depend on this.

A brand is valuable because it takes a lot of effort to create, and also to preserve. Once damaged, a brand is very difficult to repair. As a corporate example, Enron is a brand-name that became impossible to use after the exposure of extensive accounting fraud brought down the energy company in 2001.[1] The collapse was all the more spectacular because Enron had built up a strong (but false) brand identity, for instance winning *Fortune* magazine's award for "most innovative company in America" for six years running until 2000. The earlier branding helped the company to become, in its heyday, the darling of the stock market and the international business media. But after its dramatic downfall, there was no hope of brand recovery.

Countries are not like companies

By contrast, countries are different from companies in more ways than one. First, "brand-building" is a closely related term to "branding" that applies more to a country brand than a commercial one. Brand-building can refer to actions to enhance a country brand that are less overt, broader in scale and longer-term in perspective, and more often without, or with much less, upfront dollar cost. Sometimes, the effect can be subconscious, or even unconscious. For example, if a government buys an advertisement in a magazine to promote tourism, that is nation branding. If, at the same time, the government organises activities to engage citizens in events such as national celebrations of independence, that would be nation brand-building, if only indirectly. As flags are waved amidst the celebrations, some national values would be highlighted, and these are invariably the country's "brand attributes" displayed for the world to see.

Fostering national identity is key to enhancing the capacity of ordinary citizens to act as brand ambassadors for their countries, if only indirectly. Just as capitalism works through individuals being motivated in the first instance by the profit motive for personal gain, citizens who aspire to make a mark in the world (as a YouTube musician, for example) always add to the brand value of the countries they represent, whether they intend to do so or not, and in however small a way. Indeed, in the longer term, a place that seeks to be a global city would be much better-placed to achieve this goal if more people in that place understand what a nation brand is, have thought about the concept of nation branding, and have considered the possibility of their own contribution to the country brand. Such nation brand-building efforts led by the state also have an external dimension that involves public diplomacy – essentially winning friends and influencing people in the international arena. A cocktail party for foreign diplomats is not what most people would call "branding", but it is almost certainly part of "brand-building". For convenience, in this book, the term "branding" will be used for short, most of the time, even when it sometimes is actually mostly "brand-building".

Next, a country is much more multifaceted than any company, so that it is much more difficult for a country to have its brand completely destroyed. Even the most unattractive place has some redeeming feature. War-torn Afghanistan might currently rank near, or at the bottom of, all possible holiday destinations, but give it time and anything could happen, just as tourism and investment have returned to places previously ravaged by natural disaster, from hurricane-swept New Orleans to tsunami-hit Phuket. For nation branding, time can heal almost all wounds. In the Asian region, Japan offers one of the best examples of brand recovery, from the nadir of its World War II expansionism to the popularity today, across affluent Asia and elsewhere, of all things Japanese, from Tokyo's Tsukiji market (before it relocated in 2018) to winter wonderland vacations in Hokkaido. Brand Japan regularly tops global rankings such as the Country Brand Index.

Conversely, for cities or countries, unlike corporations, it is more difficult to change names and start all over again. This is not to say that changing names is not attempted from time to time. Examples include a city like Bombay renaming itself Mumbai, or a country like Myanmar relocating its entire capital from the heritage-rich Yangon to the remote Naypyi-daw, a move that accentuated its negative branding of secrecy under a military junta government in the eyes of international observers.[2] But starting over is not as daunting as it might seem, at first. The many Eastern European nations that used to be part of the former Soviet Union were given a new lease of life with the demise of communism in Europe after the fall of the Berlin Wall in 1989. For these new nations, the task of brand-building had to begin with working at dissociating themselves from any negative branding left over from the Soviet era.

Indeed, in the branding game, Russia, the nation most closely associated with the former Soviet mindset, is ironically the most successful among the former members of the Soviet Union in distancing itself from that past. First, it already had top-of-mind recall. Partly, Russia has more resources and the advantage of size. Also, it has a good springboard, building on its status as a BRICS country (part of the grouping of Brazil, Russia, India, China and South Africa as the world's five most promising up-and-coming economies[3]). In December 2010, Russia clinched another most valuable prize in nation brand-ing platforms by winning the bid to host the soccer World Cup 2018. It drew in help from internationally well-known bid ambassadors such as national soccer team captain Andrey Arshavin, who at that time played for Arsenal Football Club in the English Premier League. At the same time, develop-ments like Russia's annexation of Crimea in 2014 and reports of Russian interference in the 2016 US election have also moved Russia down a few notches in international estimation. Overall, however, Russia's success shows that countries are more resilient than corporations in branding.

Over a shorter time-span, the United States is a prominent recent example of the ups and downs that a country brand can go through. The USA's country branding was damaged during the Bush administration from 2000 to 2008, mainly due to actions taken for the "war on terror" in the Middle East, after the 911 attacks in the US in 2001. Brand America – the world's most powerful nation brand – was then rebuilt under President Barack Obama from 2008 to 2016, with a greater openness to the world, including a "pivot to Asia". But under Donald Trump, with all the missteps of the first term of his administration, with new signs every day of damaging brand attributes including withdrawal from global multilateralism, disregard of the rule of law, divisiveness, protectionism, racism and xenophobia, global perceptions of brand America have nose-dived further. By mid-2020, with the US leading the world in Covid-19 deaths and reeling from record job losses, brand America had sunk to a new low. In a much-quoted line, Fintan O'Toole of *The Irish Times* wrote: "The world has loved, hated and envied the US. Now, for the first time, we pity it."[4]

Brand recovery depends, to a large extent, on target audiences forgetting any negative branding in some measure. In the days before the Internet, there was at least amnesia to fall back on. Except for the most heinous of crooks, one could be forgiven one's misdeeds if enough time had passed; branding could rebuild all but the most devastated reputations. Today, on the one hand, it is a lot harder to hope that people will forget, because stuff that is online stays there for much, much longer and, worst of all, anyone can just "Google it".

That said, on the other hand, this effect is tempered to a large degree by another phenomenon in the way that public opinion is formed in the world today. The information may be all out there, but most people are too lazy or too busy to do their own homework. People will look something up only if they are prompted to. Instead, what happens is that they come to depend – almost entirely in some cases – on habitual sources of information. This leads to the infamous "bubbles" in which more and more people live today. These "echo chambers", in which anything they might disagree with is blocked out, is where people get their sense of the outside world. Hearsay from friends, family, Facebook feeds and even fake news crowds out facts, in what has been called a new "post-truth" universe. Hence, people can stay generally ignorant of both good and bad developments. They can remain ignorant of new successes just as much as they can stay oblivious to fresh scandals.

Nonetheless, this qualification aside, online citations remain crucial for any brand, including nation brands. The things that are cited about any brand on the first few pages of a Google search get an unimaginable amount of "multiplier effect" dissemination and reinforcement. Hence, getting good stuff about yourself onto the first page of a Google search has become paramount. The trick is how to get it there.

The Google trick

This Google trick – of influencing what is said about your brand on a Google search, or what comes up top in such searches – is even harder to pull off when it comes to nation branding. When anyone Googles your country, they can see whatever is relevant online, which adds up to what is sometimes called "digital identity". For a country seeking to do better in the world, of the three basic economic factors of production, land can usually be increased only with land reclamation, ever since imperialism went out of fashion, in a manner of speaking. The other two factors – labour and capital – will come your way only if you not only do the right things, but also do the right branding.

Nation branding is the lifeblood of any nation; it helps to attract physical and financial investments, business, trade, tourism and other economic inputs, as much as it boosts talented human resources, permanent residents and new citizens. In the global "war" for talent, resources and financing, the nations that succeed are those that can best maximise their aspects of *competitive* advantage on top of *comparative* advantage.[5] Comparative advantage – the economic concept that shows that every nation can benefit from free trade, if it can produce goods and services at a lower opportunity cost than that of its trade partners – allows small economies like Singapore to make up for the disadvantages of being small. Singapore has leveraged this well, even without producing many goods and services itself, but mostly through effective management of transshipment. It has honed this advantage further over more than 200 years as an important international trading post since the arrival in 1819 of Sir Stamford Raffles and the East India Company from Britain. Singapore is among the nations with the most extensive networks of free trade agreements – 25 by August 2020: 14 bilateral pacts and 11 regional ones. As former Foreign Minister George Yeo famously said: "Our best strategy, both for Singapore and for Asean, is to be 'completely promiscuous' in our relationships."[6] But to stay perennially ahead of the global competition, something else is needed to go one step further and add yet another extra edge, for distinctive brand differentiation. Other things being equal, the nations that can do nation branding better will gain this added *competitive* advantage.

Singapore bought into this idea with gusto. Since becoming independent in 1965, the republic has done better than many other countries in this brand space, in terms of conscious and concerted branding – albeit mainly at the sub-brand level rather than one all-encompassing, centrally directed brand. This book examines Singapore's track record in branding both internally and externally: who has tried to do what, to what effect, and where does the nation stand now in its ambitions to be Asia's leading global city. Throughout, the focus will be on how successful the state's efforts have been in influencing brand reception by Singapore's main target audiences, which include the country's own people as well as people all over the world in key areas including trade, investment, tourism, immigration, cultural exchange and international relations.

As a country, you can be paradise on Earth, but it's no good at all if no one knows. The brand messages have to be conceptualised, put together and delivered well, and get through to the target audience. This is where a brand is different from an identity. Identity is character, a set of characterisations that flesh out someone or something. This becomes a brand only when effort is put in to communicate it to target audiences, and to sustain this messaging over time. The next level would be when audiences recognise and remember the brand. And the highest level would be universal top-of-mind brand awareness. Getting the brand messaging through to the audience is where most of the attention is focused in nation branding, as with all branding. And this is no simple task.

Brand affinity: How sweet is your brand?

After brand awareness comes brand affinity, the extent to which audiences not only know about a brand, but feel positively towards it. A man who is wooing a woman must first make sure she knows his name, and then he must make her like him. Human minds are highly susceptible to influence, and yet, frustratingly hard to change. The brain works in strange ways, and often, the subconscious is thought of as being more powerful than the conscious mind. In most cultures, the sight of a snake immediately strikes fear in the beholder even when it is generally a harmless species, whereas a teddy bear evokes affection, even though real-life bears are more dangerous than cuddly. Mental models are what frame how people see and interpret reality.

This is why something like, say, wearing a turban is a symbol of social status in some cultures – as in large parts of Asia and the Middle East – but may be seen as strange and even suspicious outside that region, especially in a post-911 world.[7] It would take a rebranding effort to alter perceptions of snakes and turbans. For turbans, a recent game-changing example is the very diverse 2015 Cabinet of Canadian Prime Minister Justin Trudeau, which was hailed as "the world's most Sikh Cabinet" with four Sikh members, when even India had only two Sikh Ministers.[8]

Conversely, brand-building messages are more effective when delivered by people with appearances that are considered attractive. Messages conveyed by physically attractive people – like a blonde bombshell or a handsome, tanned hunk or a salt-and-pepper-haired gentleman in a handsome suit – are perceived better by target audiences, even though the messages could be false or the messengers completely fake.

Such mental frameworks are the products of the whole gamut of one's formative encounters with the world – upbringing, psychology, culture, history, geography, education, life experiences, familiarity with social media, and so on. The most successful branding and rebranding efforts manage to tap into this layer of subconsciousness in the brain and to influence it, just as much as they create emotive connections with the heart. Branding advocates don't borrow the military expression "battle for hearts and minds"[9] for nothing. And the order in which those twin elements are usually mentioned is important – hearts, then minds. You must touch, and win over, the heart first before you can claim a place in, and affect, the mind.

So, perhaps William Shakespeare was wrong when he wrote in his play *Romeo and Juliet* that "a rose by any other name would smell as sweet". Actually, roses smell sweet mostly thanks to branding, to the largely subconscious perceptions evoked in all onlookers as a result of everything that has ever been said and imagined about this flower, the ultimate symbol of romance. If roses were renamed, say, "rubbish", their sweetness could not but be affected, surely. It would be impossible to wish away all the negative associations around the word "rubbish". Word association is much more than an after-dinner parlour game. Human beings make sense of any external stimulus by first connecting emotively with that stimulus, and then working it out into a kind of subconscious "narrative" in the mind, stringing together the "threads" that link all the "stories" about a certain subject over time. Branding facilitates the shaping of that narrative of heart and mind. This is what branding consultants are trying to get at when they ask a client: "So what do you think is your brand story?"

Often, even those who are trying to brand themselves are not quite sure who they really are or what they want to be. They cannot articulate their own "brand story" without some help because they lack the mode of thinking and the technical vocabulary – or just any vocabulary – to describe how they really think and feel. Also, they first have to identify, and extract, this "brand essence" from deep within their own subconscious, even as, in imagining the effect of their brand, they are attempting the mammoth task of trying to read the mind of not just one other person, but in many cases, millions of people whom they have never met and will never meet. In this process, the aim is to distil and fully appreciate the "brand attributes" of a brand – that handful of key characteristics that you would like your customers to immediately think of, and which you want always to be known for.

So, in determining the "sweetness" of any brand, contrary to what Shakespeare wrote, names do mean a lot. This is why people spend so much time and money trying to come up with smart names and taglines, slogans, mottos and hashtags. If consumer branding is tough work, branding becomes even more complex when it covers an entire nation, with all its components and complexities, and when what you are trying to influence is the whole galaxy of perceptions (hearts) and opinions (minds) in the rest of the world. There is no way that anyone can go around the world and control what people think and feel about their country – that would be mission impossible. Hence, for control freaks working in country branding, much patience is asked for.

Nonetheless, people try, and some succeed. Nation branding involves actions to build the international reputation of a country, including applying to that country a combination and adaptation of the promotional techniques usually used in the business world to build a corporate image. What is needed, though, are not sexy advertisements or fancy public relations alone, but credible statements produced and disseminated consistently. When this is achieved, over time, the country earns the kind of reputation that is closer to what the owners of that brand would hope for. For example, Barack Obama, in his first few years as US president, did an almost single-handed nation-branding "job" of repairing the international image of America. Brand America had been battered between 2000 and 2008 under the Bush administration with its antagonistic handling of the global "war on terror". Obama's winning the Nobel Peace Prize after his first year on the job was a great, if debatable, personal accolade, but, more importantly, it added tremendously to the nation branding of America. The USA moved up from seventh place in 2008 to top in 2009 and 2010 in the Anholt-GfK Roper Nation Brands Index, which measures the global image of 50 nations. This nation branding turnaround for the USA was achieved not through paid advertisements in magazines and other media, but mainly through independent news coverage and citations by other people who reported and commented on what Mr Obama said and did. In the 2016 Nation Brands Index, the USA hung on to its top spot but suffered a significant drop in its score, closing the gap with second-placed Germany. It remains to be seen what ultimate damage the Trump presidency will have on the USA's nation brand rankings.

Public diplomacy and brand ambassadors

Public diplomacy – a subset of all the actions under the umbrella of nation branding – includes protecting the country's reputation and making friends with other nations, something that diplomats try to do on a daily basis. If other countries like the country you represent, they can become your external "brand ambassadors", to help shape the opinions of *other* nations about your country. But this will happen only if they generally agree with, and buy into, what you believe. What is said about Obama can work only when the images generated resonate with the existing perceptions and mental models in people's minds. But sustaining brand recognition is tough even for an Obama, as the "Obama effect" was already beginning to wane towards the end of his first term, and some observers identified this as a factor for the USA dropping off the top of some country brand rankings by

2010.[10] In the runup to the 2020 presidential election, how-ever, Obama is making a bit of a comeback in his endorse-ment of the candidacy of his former Vice President, Joe Biden.

People are more likely to form or change their opin-ions on the testimony of people they consider their friends, and on the basis of new input from sources they trust and like. This is not to say that nation branding does not work through advertisements, but that it must do much more than that. Singapore built a formidable international reputation of a modern metropolis moving in one generation from a Third World backwater to having First World living stand-ards based on most indicators. It is one of the best examples of a nation that boosted its country brand on the back of a sustained programme of concerted investment over many years in targeted advertising – complete with clever taglines, glossy photos and snazzy layouts – in leading media platforms ranging from the *Financial Times* newspaper to *Businessweek* magazine. These ads have ranged from the broad call to multinational companies to locate their business activities in the famously pro-business republic to more specific seasonal tourism promotional efforts such as the "Christmas in the Tropics" campaign that the Singapore Tourism Board held for many years from 2002.

Such ads work only if the underlying reality can support the claims made. Singapore has an excellent track record of staying within the boundaries of credibility – never claiming to be too much more than what you really are – but there still remains the formidable obstacle of lack of awareness and ingrained skepticism in target audiences. This is why, most of the time, effective nation branding is closer to public relations than advertising, working best through attracting third-party endorsement, influencing and engaging prominent media platforms off-the-record behind the scenes, and winning over key opinion leaders. If you say you're great, it is usually going to be only of so much use. But if other people say you're great, then you have something going.

Third-party endorsement: The holy grail of branding

Top-level third-party endorsement, then, is the holy grail of branding. By way of illustration, in November 2010, Singapore "arrived" on the international fashion scene, to some observers. To mark its expanding retail presence in Singapore, one of the top Italian fashion houses, Salvatore Ferragamo, launched a new necktie featuring the Merlion motif, and caused a small stir in local fashion circles. The website *CNNGo* hailed the fashion event as a signal that the "half-lion, half-fish" national motif had been accepted as a "style icon".[11] This, the online travel magazine declared, meant that there was now a "fashionably acceptable way to wear your national pride" after some four decades. It was as if the Merlion could at last hold its head up high – even if it could never have the weight of history or the authority of authentic art possessed by the most successful symbols of other nations, like the Statue of Liberty in New York City.[12] But the impact of the fashion world's acceptance of the Merlion could only be limited, until the tie could be made available and marketed beyond this special creation sold exclusively in Singapore. To begin with, the writer of the *CNNGo* article, as well as other journalists and bloggers on the subject of the Ferragamo tie, could not help but acknowledge that the Merlion symbol *per se* is typically seen as "anything but cool". Ambivalent attitudes towards this symbol of Singapore also surfaced in media observations that the Merlion looked all right only when used in such a small size, and also because it was accompanied by other, presumably less questionable motifs, namely the republic's national flower, the Papilionanthe Miss Joaquim orchid hybrid, and the traveller's palm, a familiar tropical tree in the region. Such common perceptions reflect an aspect of insecurity and awkwardness about the country's brand identity that affects and underlies almost everything that Singapore does in the sphere of nation branding. Chapter 5 explores this problematic relationship in greater detail.

The brand of a nation is called a "country brand" or "nation brand", to distinguish it from "national brand", which refers to the brand-name of a consumer product that is big enough to be distributed and recognised nationally, that is, across a whole country. Nation branding is still usually seen as a relatively new discipline. Simon Anholt, the British policy adviser and author, is credited as the pioneer of this field, and he first used the term "nation branding" in 1996 and published it in 1998 in an article titled "Nation brands of the twenty-first century" in the *Journal of Brand Management*. In December 2009, Anholt was awarded the Nobels Colloquia Prize for Leadership in Economics and Management – judged by a committee of 10 Nobel Laureates in Economics – "for his pioneering work on understanding and managing the identity and image of nations, cities and regions; and the impact of reputation on their prosperity and competitiveness". The world has seen little more than two decades of nation branding as a formal discipline. And yet, one could say that while the term "nation branding" still has the ring of the new, the activity itself has actually been practised for a much longer time in the history of man. For example, Genghis Khan (1162–1227), founder of the Mongol empire that once stretched from China across to eastern Europe, would not have been so successful a world conqueror if he had not "branded" himself as a powerful leader of fearsome warriors. The way he fought his battles was a show of force that must have struck fear into his enemies and demoralised subsequent victims of his conquests, through hearsay over countless campfires, even before his arrival. They must have known him by reputation, and been made aware of the Mongol empire by a process much like nation branding, long before the term was invented.

Brand equity: Nothing like a good story

The accumulated store of brand awareness and affinity becomes what is called "brand equity". Place branding work builds brand equity, like a reservoir of positive perception and goodwill in the minds and hearts of customers, much the same way that financial wealth is acquired and kept in reserve in the bank for future spending. In the meantime, this equity is the stock on which credit is accorded by customers to a brand.

Or, one could use the language of military conquest to describe how market share is won. Today, nation branding conquers territory in much more benign ways than Genghis Khan's invasions, although it may even have become more "aggressive", if in a totally different way. In 2009, the "Best Job in the World" campaign by Queensland Tourism in Australia invited people around the world to apply for a dream job as "caretaker" of Hamilton Island and to get paid doing it – a salary of A$150,000. The campaign was dubbed "the world's greatest PR stunt",[13] and it created a tremendous positive side-effect of nation branding for Australia as a whole, enhancing perceptions of the country as being fun, relaxed and close to nature. The viral effect of people all over the world telling their friends about this job opportunity via online social media was very powerful – attracting over 34,000 video entries from applicants in 200 countries, and more than 7 million visitors to the website submitting nearly 500,000 votes. This happened largely because the prize reinforced most people's mental pictures of what paradise on Earth would be like: sunny skies, blue waters, nothing much to do but laze around, and with the bonus of a salary at the end of it, to boot. The key to it all was that the Hamilton Island campaign had the critical success factor that any branding effort needs at its heart: a good story.

The most successful nation branding happens when a brand attribute that is being advertised or highlighted squares with perceived reality. This can move both ways, however. The highs attained for international perceptions of Australia drawn from the "Best Job in the World" campaign in 2009 contrasted with the lows seen just a year later, when Australia was slammed for apparently revealing its true colours as a "pariah state" after news broke of racist attacks on foreign students of Indian ethnicity in 2010.[14] This aspect surfaced again in 2020 during the Covid-19 pandemic with reported displays of racism against people of Chinese ethnicity, triggered by news of the association with Wuhan, China, as the place of origin of this strand of coronavirus.

Nation branding is a particularly tricky form of marketing, because the country brand is not just one product, but a vast amalgam of any and all of the many disparate elements that make up a nation, and a country brand can be damaged at any time by forces quite beyond the control of those handling its nation branding efforts. In most countries, a pack of wildcards that gets thrown into the fray comes in the form of aspects of internal branding that are difficult to manage. From the government's point of view, these potentially disruptive forces include political divisiveness, an antagonistic media and a restless and demanding public. The "divided states" of America under a Trump presidency might present just such a challenging scenario, which will make it difficult for internal cohesiveness, an important first ingredient for a strong nation brand. Singapore, however, is an example of a country in which these elements play a strictly limited role, in some cases for unique reasons, as the rest of this book will discuss in more detail.

While nation brand-building is ultimately about reputation, or how a country looks to the outside world, there is an important internal, or domestic, dimension, which is often neglected by policymakers. Internal branding, then, is the way the country brand is communicated to, and shaped in the minds of, the citizens of that country – the people who are, or are supposed to be, "living the brand". This is analogous to the way that a company or product brand is promoted to the employees of that corporation, something that is also often overlooked by the management. Thus, a company that prides itself on top-quality products must first convince its own employees of the key brand attributes as applied to its corporate vision, core values, processes, standards and norms.

In the case of Singapore, its internal nation branding has been extraordinarily successful in cultivating brand attributes such as cohesiveness, although it has been less effective in other aspects such as creativity. For example, in implementing any major shift in national priorities – such as the 180-degree U-turn in policy from the complete ban on casinos before 2004 to an all-out promotion of the "integrated resorts" that house the two casinos – the country as a whole is brought along in this shift in the economy, while critics and detractors are mainly left by the wayside. This may go some way towards explaining the republic's external branding achievements in its international positioning, highlighting brand attributes ranging from political stability to administrative efficiency to public safety that are founded on the capability for mostly unchallenged policy adjustments, coordinated action and swift mobilisation of resources, with predictable, reliable follow-through.

The power of internal nation branding can be illustrated by the following example. The Singapore flag has two equal horizontal bands – red on top and white below – with a crescent moon and five stars in white at the top left. In the mind of the average Singapore citizen, as a result of years of national education in school, the new moon is always thought to represent "a young nation". Most Singaporeans are quite startled when it is pointed out to them for the first time that a crescent moon is also the unmistakable international symbol of Islam, something that is in their general knowledge. But the idea of Singapore being "an Islamic nation" is a thought they have been conditioned not to entertain.

This predominance of the "young nation" idea in a powerful context of secularism has been made possible only because, in a system and culture of instinctive deference to authority, augmented by censorship and self-censorship, one little slice of history has been so seldom mentioned until recently. When the flag was being designed in 1965 by a committee headed by Toh Chin Chye,[15] then the deputy prime minister, the crescent moon was something the Malay-Muslim population wanted, whereas the five stars on a red background were suggested by Chinese Singaporeans because these are elements on the national flag of China.

This piece of historical trivia is now included on a National Heritage Board website,[16] but many Singaporeans remain ignorant of the origins of their own national flag. A cohesive following internally is certainly useful for external nation branding efforts, and few nations can do social cohesiveness quite like Singapore. Having so many internal brand ambassadors in the citizens, and such avid ones at that, may be a vital part of the secrets of success for a country aiming to be Asia's leading global city, even through and beyond the Covid-19 pandemic. The effectiveness of Singapore's internal nation branding is, to begin with, a testament to the power and influence of state actors in the process of nation branding – something that the next chapter explores.

CHAPTER 2

STATE OF PLAY

The government's "visible hand"
in nation branding

ITHOUT NATION BRANDING, there would be no Singapore. With the Covid-19 pandemic, this is now all the more so. When self-government was attained in 1959, Singapore's country brand was unimpressive, to say the least. In the words of Dr Albert Winsemius, the Dutch economist who led a United Nations team to advise the new city-state on its economic development in 1960, and remained an adviser until 1984, if Singapore had been a car, it was "a lemon, not a Rolls-Royce".[1] Turning a lemon into a Rolls-Royce essentially sums up the rest of Singapore's history of economic growth to date, with nation branding playing a crucial role.

Brand Singapore

After 1961, with the establishment of the Economic Development Board (EDB), the lead agency to attract foreign investment, the main effort was focused on what the EDB calls its day-to-day work: "investment promotion". But essentially it all hinged on nation branding, because Singapore's sole aim was to attract foreign investment, and the country had practically nothing else to go on. There were no natural resources to speak of, the workforce was mostly untrained, the domestic market was negligible and the hinterland politically unstable. In the EDB's 40th-anniversary book *Heart Work* (2002), Chan Chin Bock, former EDB chairman, recalled that every conversation he had with a potential investor in the 1970s was a sales pitch about Singapore's value propositions. He was acting like a salesman, "selling" Singapore as a place to relocate manufacturing activity. Unknowingly, he was also doing nation branding. He had been instructed by Finance Minister Goh Keng Swee to organise a plant-opening ceremony every day, if possible, to make headlines, build the confidence of investors and create a critical mass in each industry sector. What Chan did was to have *two* ceremonies for each company – one when a project was committed and a second when production actually started. In those early days, it was as if almost any investment would do: Among the companies that received pioneer certificates – granting them access to tax and other incentives – were those making mosquito coils and household locks.

From the earliest days, the EDB approach, focused on

nation branding, was applied in attracting investments mostly from the developed economies in North America, western Europe and Japan. From the 21st century onwards, the catchment regions expanded to new geographies including the Middle East, eastern Europe and the Asia-Pacific. The range of target industries has also widened from the previous focus on manufacturing and manufacturing-related services to now include a much bigger range of services and other industry sectors, from digital animation to lifestyle products. A secondary effort was to attract selected individuals as well, those who would bring with them high-value economic activity. While the "infantry" of EDB officers knocked on doors every day around the world, "air cover" was provided by strategic advertising in leading business media, with taglines like this: "Singapore is pro-business; that's why business is pro-Singapore".

Over the years, like any commercial branding outfit, adaptability to customer needs was key. The kind of branding proposition that would convince an electronics company like Hewlett-Packard to build factories and regional offices in a place like Singapore in the 20th century – such as fulfilling precise specifications – is qualitatively different from what would clinch the deal in the 21st century for a digital animation company like Lucasfilm of the *Star Wars* movie franchise fame – such as improvising to enhance the product even further. But one thing has not changed: At the heart of every EDB officer's work has always been nation branding, pure and simple. This spirit has been successfully transferred into, and embedded in, other public service officers in other agencies, such as International Enterprise Singapore, the trade promotion body helping Singapore-based companies to regionalise and globalise their operations, that was renamed Enterprise Singapore in 2018 after merging with another agency, Spring Singapore, looking after startups and smaller companies. Even other government bodies have imbibed and applied this nation branding focus, including, for instance, the Ministry of Health when it promotes Singapore in seeking to attract doctors to relocate to the Lion City to help boost its healthcare capabilities.

Why is the nation building and branding experience of this small patch of land of so much interest to the world? Well, the reasons are many. International visitors to Singapore, especially those from aspiring developing countries, routinely ask about the country's secrets of success, in aspects such as public housing, where the majority (more than 80 per cent) of the resident population live, unlike in most other countries. Singapore's public housing is a testament to what is possible with policy commitment from the start to high-rise, high-density living, and then to making this as liveable as possible. As early as 1992, Singapore's Housing and Development Board had received the United Nations' World Habitat Award in the developed country category for Tampines town as an innovative and successful human settlement. Successful innovations have been implemented in many other areas. Singapore may have a population of around 5.7 million, including all foreigners, but it is consistently regarded among the world's top five most competitive economies, according to the pre-eminent global ranking of national competitiveness by the Switzerland-based World Economic Forum. In the WEF Global Competitiveness Index 2019, Singapore ranked top as the world's most competitive economy, overtaking the USA.[2] The Lion City has been the top Asian country on this ranking for many years. Singapore has long been held up as a role model for developing countries, for them to see what lessons they can apply to their own situations, to try to emulate Singapore's remarkable success story of building its per capita income from around US$500 in the 1960s to over US$50,000 by 2015 – in short, progressing from Third World to First World status in economic terms in just one generation.

This track record is spoken of with some admiration for the unexpected scale and speed of economic advancement, something that many nations still can only dream of.[3] Much of this success has come from the country's ability to keep attracting and retaining foreign investment from multinational manufacturers, financial sector firms, entrepreneurs and other players. Nation branding has been deeply integral to this effort since the 1960s. Indeed, this kind of nation branding – specifically customised for the key target audience of high-net-worth investors both institutional and individual – is something that is worked and reworked on a daily basis by hundreds, if not more, of politicians, policy-makers and public servants involved in economic planning and promotion, diplomats, researchers and others in Singapore.

Despite what may seem to outside observers as a highly coordinated "government machinery", country branding in Singapore is actually executed mostly at the sub-brand level of trade, investment, tourism and immigration. On a daily basis, the impact on the nation brand is quite often indirect – that is, the effort in any particular initiative may be intended as external marketing per se rather than brand-building, or for domestic socio-political or other purposes. What brings everyone together is a common goal of developing the economy. Since the 2000s, much of the external marketing of Singapore has been focused around catalysing economic activity with an ingredient called "vibrancy", for want of a better word. One favourite buzzword in the civil service is "vibrant". Each day, hundreds of public service officers crack their heads to see what else they can do to add to Singapore's "vibrancy", in whichever sphere of work they are involved in, from Foreign Ministry officers crafting another cultural event to reach for a new level of quintessential Singaporeanness to impress their foreign counterparts in some far-flung corner of the globe to Singapore Land Authority officers dreaming up another ground-breaking type of use for a plot of state land that can be developed into another "identity node" such as a "little Bohemia", to create a business and social environment for a modern, hip lifestyle that is also rich in heritage in selected localities around the island.[4]

The "GDP city"

All this nation branding work is focused single-mindedly on one end in mind. Singapore is sometimes affectionately called "a fine city", with a pun on its reputation for fines for everything from littering to jay-walking. But the country might as well also be called the "GDP city" for the way that almost every public-policy decision is geared towards boosting the gross domestic product. National resources are pooled for the government to "bet on the right horses" – those sunrise industries working on "the next big thing" that will add the most to the GDP. Almost every other aspect of life contributes to this. Vehicle road use is taxed heavily to keep the gears of the economy running. Talented new citizens are prized primarily for their economic value. Cabinet ministers' and top civil servants' salary increases and performance bonuses are pegged to the fluctuations of the GDP. Even the arts are promoted primarily to help boost economic competitiveness, either as an industry in its own right, or as a helpful ingredient of "vibrant" city life to attract high-net-worth individuals. The financial and economic connotations of favourite Singaporean terms such as "cultural capital" and "creative industries" are fully intended. Something that has been honed to such a degree for so many years, with so much time, brainpower and other resources invested to such success in nation branding terms, must hold some intriguing learning points for anyone interested in this subject.

Brand Singapore

For a country that has known only one-party-dominant rule for the whole of its sovereign existence since 1965 – indeed, as far back as 1959 when the British granted the city self-government – it is perhaps only natural that the state has had the biggest hand in nation branding as well. At the command of the authorities are not only aspects such as having a mandate to govern that is fully embraced by those in power, immense resources and strategic international networks and linkages, but also a culture of followership in everyone else taking the cue from those in charge. Among more developed nations, Singapore may be unique in the extent to which the people have given the government the mandate to be the overall brand steward and primary actor. This is in contrast to a country like the USA, where "brand America" is projected at home and abroad with equal, if not more, autonomous vision and vigour by corporate actors and individuals compared with government agents. Hence, someone like film director Steven Spielberg has much freedom and power in adding to the USA's nation branding with the movies he makes, because of the enormous reach and influence of Hollywood. The American government would have to lobby Hollywood if it wished to affect what was being conveyed onscreen about brand America. Singapore, by contrast, has nothing like a Hollywood or Microsoft. So, the Singapore government steps in to take direct control of the job of brand guardianship, at least from the perspectives of spending public money and coordinating official communication in this effort.

A clean and smart nation

Overall, Singapore's government agencies' record in nation branding has been very good, even if the brand outcomes were achieved without consciously and directly applying the techniques of branding. There are many strengths with deep roots – such as the "Garden City" branding, which was deliberately sown in the 1960s by the prime minister then, Lee Kuan Yew, to impress potential foreign investors that their investments would be maintained as diligently as well-trimmed hedges and manicured lawns.[5] And, just as a beautiful garden is always the result of careful tending and hours of toil, Singapore's most admired brand attributes did not, by any means, come about by accident.

Singapore has always had a high ranking within the global top 10 for lack of corruption in assessments by the Berlin-based Transparency International, for example, coming in fourth in 2019 out of 180 countries, the only Asian nation in the top 10.[6] This zero-tolerance stand on corruption since the 1960s has become such a social norm that no Singaporean would dream of trying to bribe a traffic cop (which is illegal), and the system is well-accepted to have comparatively high salaries for political office-holders benchmarked to the private sector's top earners, among other reasons, as a deterrent to kickbacks. The country's clean reputation is the fruit of two main factors: one is the "big stick" of swift action and severe penalties by agencies such as the Corrupt

Practices Investigation Bureau (CPIB)[7] and Commercial Affairs Department (CAD)[8]; and the second is the peer pressure of a general culture of aversion to any kind of bribery, embezzlement or other financial misdemeanour. The first factor has contributed to nation branding in a crucial way. In 1995, Nick Leeson was a British trader at Barings in Singapore when his falsified transactions of up to 8 billion yen (about US$95 million at today's rates) brought down Britain's oldest merchant bank, the equivalent of a Lehman Brothers debacle of an earlier decade. But although the corporate brand-name Barings was destroyed after that episode – much like Lehman Brothers' would be more than a decade later – Singapore's country brand not only did not suffer, but instead grew much stronger in trustworthiness, for its corporate governance and financial system management, as seen in the way that the case was handled by the CAD and the government with speed, efficiency and integrity.

Indeed, Singapore's good standing in the area of law enforcement has been further boosted by other developments, such as the prominent position held by former Singapore Police Force Commissioner Khoo Boon Hui serving as the president of Interpol (2008–2012), the organisation that facilitates international police cooperation among nearly 200 countries. Singapore's reputation for sticking closely to rules and procedures might be irksome to those of a more maverick bent, but mostly, it has added much to its nation branding. Being known for being good with things like governance and compliance has contributed to the city-state's strong standing as a financial centre. This put Singapore in good stead amid the global financial crisis of 2008, and in the recovery phase thereafter, helping the republic become one of the fastest-recovering economies worldwide by 2010. Such brand equity, built and sustained over decades, will surely be a valuable asset in the recovery from the Covid-19 pandemic.

On top of the "hard" aspects, such as laws against corruption, there are also "soft" factors that have accounted for Singapore's good name among nations. All are areas that have seen focused priority and promotion by the government. One of these is the extensive use of English as the main language of administration and business. This is something that did not come naturally to a heterogeneous society. It was government policy from the start to adopt the colonial tongue as the main working language, so as not to be seen to favour any of the three main ethnic groups, the Chinese, Indians and Malays. This socio-political move also generated much economic payoff. A generally high level of proficiency in English, especially in the workplace, continues to be cited as a key aspect of Singapore's competitive edge against its rivals such as Hong Kong in the past and China more recently, although this edge may be diminishing as other countries are catching up on this factor. It is an area that the government has invested in for many years in the school system as well as through public education campaigns like the Speak Good English Movement.

This is one aspect of the legacy of British colonialism that Singapore has welcomed and wielded to its vast benefit, with typical Singaporean pragmatism.[9] The teaching of English is also, arguably, Singapore's most prominent regular regional contribution to the Association of Southeast Asian Nations (Asean), through its hosting of the Regional Language Centre, set up by Asean in 1968 to raise the standard of English for the region's economic advancement.[10] A good foundation in English also accounts for the high international standing that Singapore's education system has had for many decades. For example, in 2015, Singapore caught global attention by ranking top in the triennial Program for International Student Assessment (PISA) conducted by the Organisation for Economic Cooperation and Development (OECD). The study ranks 15-year-old students in some 70 countries on proficiency in reading, mathematics and science.[11]

Another facet is Singapore's connectivity, which has seen continued investment in wiring up all homes for faster Internet broadband speeds, as part of the Intelligent Nation 2015 masterplan, whose slogan was "A Global City, Powered by Infocomm".[12] More recently, the Smart Nation plan to make Singapore the world's first smart nation is potentially a concept that will add to the global brand differentiation of Singapore as a country brand. Many other cities are working to become smart cities but, once again, Singapore's small size and central coordination will enable it to go one better, by harnessing the benefits of technology and connectivity as an entire country. This plan aims to make Singapore a smart nation not only in the technological sense in using more sensors and big data to enhance aspects such as traffic management. There is just as much of a focus on "social connectivity" amongst citizens, for example, having a system of citizen volunteers who sign up to be contacted by smartphone to help when neighbours near their homes are in emergency situations such as suffering from a heart attack, by using automated external defibrillators located in many places. There is also the dimension of marshalling the collective efforts of businesses to apply technology to enable better living, for example, for owners of commercial buildings to enhance the security of their own premises to complement state efforts in maintaining public safety.

The tourism brand journey

To reach the widest audiences internationally, the tourism platform for nation branding remains the most widely accessed, and therefore, the most remembered and powerful. Here, Singapore's brand positioning has had several major revamps in more than five decades, steered on each occasion by those in charge of the Singapore Tourism Board,[13] and more recently, influenced also by other agencies such as those working in the Ministry of Communications and Information; the Ministry of Culture, Community and Youth; and the Ministry of Trade and Industry. These efforts are supported by other agencies in policy and implementation, from the Prime Minister's Office to the Ministry of Manpower.

Singapore's tourism promotion efforts over the years have no doubt been successful in boosting tourism arrivals and developing the country's leisure options, growing the total annual visitor arrivals to the record level of more than 19 million in 2019, before the Covid-19 pandemic brought about a sharp break in that growth trend. For people who have been to Singapore, or at least have some basic brand knowledge of the place, the country's tourism branding over the years has spoken to them in different ways. This is, in some ways, like preaching to the converted, but even so, Singapore's tourism offerings have been updated and added to, to such an extent that even local residents have begun to find it hard to keep up. But to those who hardly know Singapore, tourism branding is a different, often challenging, matter calling for really effective messaging – hence the rise of the term "brand evangelist". To this larger audience, in nation branding terms, Singapore's brand journey and positioning can certainly be analysed more deeply, to suggest aspects of missed potential for even sharper nation branding in future.

In the 1960s and 1970s, the key idea and tagline was "Instant Asia", playing on the notion of Singapore as an ideal entry-point, gateway and platform for gaining access to the major cultures, foods and festivals of Asia – all in one place. As Singapore was still shedding the vestiges of the mindset of a formerly colonised people, this was a time of a lower level of national identity and self-confidence, perhaps manifest in the less sophisticated approach to nation branding, as seen in the appeal to Western notions of "the exotic East" with a kind of "self-Orientalisation" that continues to be a vestigial feature of nation branding efforts even today. While the idea of an "instant Asia" held a certain attraction in itself and was successful in getting Singapore's international tourism appeal off the ground, perhaps the brand's connotative power left something to be desired. The idea that Singapore could offer a bit of the major cultures of Asia, especially Chinese, Indian and Malay, might unwittingly have reinforced the thought that what Singapore offered was an array of "appetisers" of the major cultures, and hence, those who wanted to really appreciate the "main course" of these cultures would do better to spend more time elsewhere in Asia, such as in China, India, Malaysia or Indonesia. Perhaps at that time, the particular brand differentiation for Singapore *per se* had yet to be fully captured and articulated.

In the 1980s, the focus turned to the slogan "Surprising Singapore", as if uncovering this "surprise" was an attempt to go deeper than what the previous notion of "Instant Asia" had seemed to suggest. The idea was to seek to emphasise modernity and Asian exoticism together – again attempting nation branding with a kind of smorgasbord approach, but this time, with a narrowing focus on the menu to a type of fusion cuisine. The appeal to audiences to delve deeper into their experience of Singapore, beyond surface impressions, remains loud till today, even as the approach has become subtler and more segmented. However, once again, the tagline spoke of something closer to the superficial than the substantial. "Surprise" is something of an initial reaction, a first impression rather than a lasting one. While this might have caught people's attention and invited closer scrutiny, the brand concept again could have been sharper in zeroing in on what it is about Singapore that surprises visitors, to truly come closer to the heart of Singapore's brand essence.

In the 1990s, the "something for everyone" line was still there, when the "New Asia" concept began to draw attention to tradition-steeped ethnic cultures fused into modern development – a kind of melting pot different from, and perhaps more authentic than, what one could find in a city like New York, and yet hinting at the reinvention and modernisation going on all the time, a blend of hardware and software "to create a total experience".[14] Like many other such nation branding efforts from Singapore, the ideas in this campaign were wrapped in pairings, each attempting to tease out surprising or paradoxical word associations such as this: "Singapore has its soul in the past, but its head in the future".[15] This brand concept was an improvement on the previous two, in that it got closer to the distinctive content of the brand. But what it failed to do was to develop the paradoxical juxtapositions further to create a statement that Singapore could truly own in the crowded brand space of global destination marketing.

Moving into the 21st century, the only time that the tourism brand positioning for Singapore departed from the "all things to all men" offering was in 2005, when the "Uniquely Singapore" branding was unveiled. Although criticised in some quarters for lacking identity and substance – because "everything is unique" anyway – this branding concept actually contained a lot of potential, which unfortunately was not fully developed. There are, indeed, quite a few things that are unique about Singapore that can be used to differentiate its brand positioning from all other nations. The challenge was how to deal with several ideas all at once, since no one unifying idea was being highlighted at any one time.

"YourSingapore": Tourism DIY

In 2010, the brand proposition moved back in the opposite direction – from closing in on the unique to being all things to all men once again. This tendency might reflect a quintessential Singaporean characteristic – the urge to try to have your cake and eat it. The new tourism tagline of "YourSingapore"[16] (spelt as one word for trademark purposes) invited travellers to put together their own personal itinerary to discover Singapore and to find their own sense of the place. This was based on the insight that, in an era of the advent of selfies and Instagram moments, most travellers today, armed with smartphones encased in their favourite personal colour and design, want personalisation in their travel experience, and

51

so, prefer to customise their trips the way they like them. For the first time, digital media platforms such as Facebook and Google were used as major channels of drawing attention.

So, once again, the wheel had turned back to the "something for everyone" and "different strokes for different folks" mindset. While this approach might work for most travellers – giving them a kind of online DIY tour guide – it does miss the opportunity to offer a fresh statement of what exactly is Singapore's brand essence. In a sense, then, one could argue that this is really a kind of post-modern, "deconstructionist" way of nation branding – the brand concept has moved quite far indeed from the conventional way of pushing out a crafted message with objective "proof points", and instead, all that remains is a mechanism to pull audiences in, to discover the brand essence through multiple interpretations – leaving them to put bits and pieces together on their own terms in a personal, subjective way.

One might argue that all the direct and indirect references over the years to an underlying "buffet mentality" of trying to be all things to all men were diluting the Singapore brand all the time, and now, the dilution is, in a way, complete. This could be contrasted with the more focused and consistent nation branding of other countries such as New Zealand, with its "100% Pure New Zealand" focus on being close to nature, or Thailand, with its "Amazing Thailand" appeal to the exotic, or Malaysia, with its emphasis on authenticity with the tagline "Truly Asia". Countries like

Thailand have natural advantages such as impressive scenery and a greater critical mass of indigenous culture that Singapore can never hope to match. One could find fault with the New Zealand, Thai and Malaysian taglines too, but it must be noted that at least they are comparatively more focused on a specific quality that gives the campaign the sense of a little more substance – what branding consultants might call a branding "point of view" – that audiences can grasp easily and remember.

The brand substance of Singapore for tourism has thus proven to be elusive over the years, distracted by abstract notions such as "surprising", "new" and "unique". The Singapore Tourism Board's 2013 "Shiok" video campaign – using the Malay/Singlish adjective to describe something highly pleasurable – goes some way in capturing Singapore's brand essence. This should be the way forward. As for a key image, likening Singapore to, say, a kaleidoscope would at least give its brand identity some specific substance. To a large extent, Singapore *is* a kaleidoscope in many ways – of cultures, work and lifestyle options, and so on. Its nation branding overall is also based on much more than tourism, with a strong foundation in business infrastructure and a social and political system that has many distinctive plus points.[17] With Singapore's increasing cosmopolitanism in recent years, the kaleidoscope has turned to reveal even more sparkling dimensions than ever before.

"Passion Made Possible":
Best tourism concept

In 2017, Singapore launched its latest tourism branding around the tagline "Passion Made Possible", and it is the most effective concept thus far. The branding paradigm shift was to focus not so much on what there is to do, but what one could become, in Singapore. The key idea is that Singapore is a conducive, welcoming, happening place, where people can realise their passions in many ways. The rich, harmonious cultural heritage inspires creativity everywhere, from nurturing homegrown apparel designers to digital artists to athletes in unusual sports like indoor skydiving to chefs who experiment with ingredients from Singapore's cosmopolitan mix to excel in fusion cuisine. The innovative creations of these passionate people appeal to more sophisticated visitors with diverse interests, who might belong to "tribes" including foodies, action seekers, culture shapers, socialisers, collectors or explorers.

What sets this brand concept apart from previous campaigns are its authenticity and emotive appeal. The authenticity comes from featuring real people with real-life stories as brand ambassadors, instead of the old way of advertisements featuring actors re-enacting imagined scenes. Another key initiative was to partner with brand ambassadors in target markets. For example, a key event for the brand launch in London was a cocktail festival featuring *Straight Up*, a book on global cocktail culture including the best bars in Singapore, written by two British spirits experts, Joel Harrison and Neil Ridley. In Britain, what better way is there to connect than over drinks?

To craft this new branding, for the first time, the Singapore Tourism Board did not work alone, but together with the Economic Development Board. This concept was positioned as the "first unified brand for Singapore on the international front, built on an inside-out approach of what Singapore stands for".[18] "Inside-out" here is a branding keyword, signalling the importance of starting with a deep dive into the genuine brand substance of what is available at home, which then serves as the launch pad from which to craft a messaging for the world outside.

Despite STB and EDB collaborating in the formulation of this concept, the two agencies implemented the brand with different approaches, to connect with their very different target audiences. For EDB, the key idea was "Singapore: The Impossible Story", presenting this as "the special place for those who love proving the world wrong".[19] The brand coherence here with STB's presentation mode is in the common focus on possibilities – in EDB's case, for companies and entrepreneurs who might want to locate some economic activity in Singapore.

Now that the Covid-19 pandemic has dealt the global tourism industry a heavy blow, for Singapore, the brand equity won with almost three years of promoting the "Passion Made

Possible" and "The Impossible Story" concepts should stand the city-state in good stead as a foundation to build on, when the conditions for recovery eventually materialise.

With international travel now almost entirely stalled, STB has turned its attention to domestic tourism for the first time since the earliest days of independence. This is a priority that is so unusual that it is almost like turning to a blank slate, as detailed statistics for domestic tourism – on this small city-state that has always looked outwards to the world – had not even been properly kept previously. Nonetheless, encouraging residents to visit places of interest on the island is actually an opportunity for internal brand-building, a dimension of country branding that is typically not given the attention it deserves. For example, with clever brand positioning, visitors to, say, Gardens by the Bay could gain a deeper appreciation of the nation brand attribute of the country's openness to the world, as seen in the way that the gardens bring the world to Singapore through plants. Tourism is, indeed, moving into uncharted waters.

Culture: The quest for focused substance from "SG50"

The quest for focused substance in nation branding has motivated the interest in looking for it in what is the only realm where it can usually be found – culture. At home, in addition to cultural "products" made in Singapore, partnerships with other countries have also been part of the positioning to internal audiences of Singapore's connections with other cultures around the world, such as the celebration of all things Japanese at the 2016 Super Japan Festival at the Esplanade – Theatres on the Bay. Overseas, for international promotion of the Singapore brand, quite a lot has been done in the space of direct marketing and branding overseas through high-signature cultural platforms. Over the years, Singapore has been systematically branded in this way in strategic locations abroad.

"The Singapore Season", a series of cultural diplomacy festivals showcasing the culture of Singapore in food, theatre and other aspects, was launched in London in 2005 and staged in Beijing and Shanghai in 2007. The Singapour Festivarts festival in Paris, 2010/2011, showcased indigenous culture such as Peranakan arts. The French connection was there with the screening of Singapore films that had appeared at the Cannes Film Festival, including *Here* by Ho Tzu Nyen, which premiered at Cannes in 2009. Such events are huge efforts, just judging by the number of organisations involved. For example, Singapour Festivarts was presented by the Ministry of Information, Communications and the Arts, together with the Asian Civilisations Museum, National Arts Council, Media Development Authority and Singapore Tourism Board. The Singapore partners for the festival were Singapore Airlines and its airline catering company, three property firms and a shipping corporation.

Typically, it is often a struggle to secure coverage by international media, even in the country hosting the event.[20] Branding is nothing if not a long-haul effort, especially for smaller countries. Nonetheless, coverage by the host country's domestic media and, perhaps sometimes even more importantly, effective direct marketing and mindshare-building among key opinion leaders in that location itself can reap long-term rewards for such presentations of a foreign country's culture. After all, it was precisely due to earlier concerted nation branding efforts by Singapore – most of which drew only limited but effective coverage that inspired a few key people in the "target destination" – that led to the creation of Singapour Festivarts in the first place.

Another overseas platform is Spotlight Singapore, an international cultural and economic exchange programme, that has been held in places including Hong Kong, Tokyo, Moscow and Cape Town. The idea is to "use cultural diplomacy to open markets for Singapore companies".[21] Such events reflect a pervasive mindset of Singaporean officialdom – culture and the arts are most useful in nation branding when they can serve the cause of economic development and contribute to the GDP. The unasked question is: If and when the overseas target audiences realise this underlying utilitarian motive beneath the promotion of culture and the arts, will this affect the chances of success of the mission itself?

Supplementing "physical world" efforts such as the Singapore Season are other initiatives ongoing in the virtual world of the media, that can potentially be much more powerful in terms of reach, impact and shelf-life. In 2009, the Media Development Authority launched the Singapore Media Fusion Plan,[22] which set out three approaches to grow the media sector: to provide the best environment for media business; to leverage research and development to help the media sector exploit new opportunities in the digital media value chain; and to remain connected to the world to enhance the international appeal of Singapore-made content, applications and services. The end in mind? To transform Singapore into a "Trusted Global Capital for New Asia Media".[23] The measures taken include funding new media productions and strengthening government-to-government agreements to foster collaborations with media producers overseas.

For the visual arts, the massive game-changer has been the opening in November 2015 of the National Gallery Singapore. Housed in two magnificent colonial buildings – the former City Hall and Supreme Court – the gallery oversees more than 8,000 works that chronicle the art history of Singapore and the Southeast Asian region from the 19th century to the present day. Without being ostentatious, the gallery plays a role as a custodian and guardian of some measure of the immense artistic riches of the region, thus winning for Singapore tremendous goodwill and brand affinity that cannot be fully quantified. Internationally, the architectural and artistic prominence of the gallery will see it play a leading role at the vanguard of what the *New York Times*, for instance, has called Singapore's "new cultural vision".[24]

In the realm of cinema, Singapore hopes to become the "Cannes of Asia" with events such as the ScreenSingapore film festival, which premiered Asian films and previews of US blockbusters, and aimed to attract Hollywood's A-list glitterati.[25] Such events seek to tap opportunities in Asia as a primary source of growth in the film and entertainment business in the years to come, as and when the focus of the industry shifts from the mature American market to areas outside the US. Unfortunately for Singapore, size does matter in the media, and small countries will, in all likelihood, always struggle to challenge the market dominance of Hollywood – or even Bollywood, for that matter.

Of course, as with any branding effort, delivery of content is only part of the journey. After that, there are still the subsequent phases of *reception* by the target audience – understanding, appreciation, assessment and acceptance of the content – before there can be any follow-up action that comes anywhere near to meeting the branding objectives. While these events do make an impact, not least among foreigners directly involved in participation, organisation and reporting, the areas really requiring attention are follow-up, follow-through and following. There have been too many cultural collaboration agreements signed in the past, with territories ranging from Scotland to Egypt, that produced a few worthwhile initiatives in the immediate wake of their signing, but are since hardly heard about, and worse, whose legacy has not been properly captured and built upon. Much more could be done to nurture a following in interest areas sparked by such inter-government initiatives. For instance, an untapped resource are the numerous "alumni" of these initiatives, all those potential brand ambassadors who took part in cultural exchange programmes and events over the years, and some of them – such as artists seeking to connect with audiences – would be only too happy to help sustain or revive the collaborations.

On this score, "SG50" in 2015 – the 50th anniversary of Singapore's independence as a nation – was hugely successful for internal brand-building, but less so externally. Abroad, there was some positive spinoff for tourism, with major international media including *Lonely Planet* and the *New York Times* naming Singapore as the best place to visit in 2015. But, in the main, the year was a case of missed opportunity for external branding. Some of the countries that established diplomatic relations with Singapore 50 years ago – from its former colonial master Britain to other countries from Canada to Thailand – took the chance to mount a series of activities to promote their country brands to audiences in Singapore, with events ranging from a celebratory exhibition of Canadian literature in Singapore's public libraries to a showcase of classical Thai dance at Singapore's Victoria Theatre. These activities carried on into subsequent years. In 2016, a notable country example was Japan, which not only organised a whole year of more than 200 brand-building events including a *matsuri* (street festival) on the main shopping street Orchard Road that was closed to traffic, attracting some 110,000 people, but also used the branding of "SJ50" (signifying Singapore-Japan 50) to play off the "SG50" brand. By contrast, looking at what Singapore could have done in a reciprocal way – to build the Singapore brand in these other countries by also celebrating the 50th anniversaries of bilateral ties with activities there – it appears that there was more that could have been done.

This deficit in state-led promotion of the cultural dimensions of brand Singapore is consistent with what has been the general approach to country brand-building by Singapore since around the start of the 2010s, one that has been left on a generally "auto-pilot" mode at the overall national level of coordination. Nonetheless, Singapore's nation brand has continued, by and large, to hold its own and to grow, in spite of a lack of concerted effort coordinated centrally by the government. Instead, country brand-building has continued to be conducted in earnest in decentralised ways by separate, albeit complementary, government agencies pursuing their goals in areas such as trade, investment promotion, tourism and so on. Still, more concerted effort would certainly help to capture some of the potential in the many occasions of missed opportunity. The game-changing development is that the nation brand-building awareness and energies of the people have been mobilised by everything that happened during the

"SG50" year. This aspect will be further discussed in Chapter 4 on the people's contributions to nation branding.

Harvesting the fruit of the "Garden City" model

Of all the brand propositions in five decades of government-led nation branding, perhaps the strongest one has been that of Singapore as a "Garden City". Being the earliest brand proposition that caught on from the 1960s, it has the endurance of a first impression, at least among people above a certain age. Many public sector officials and researchers from overseas have visited Singapore to learn how the city of orchids does things like plant creepers and bougainvillea shrubs along concrete flyovers, or transplant exotic trees and trim hedges seemingly at every street corner and road divider. Pavan Sukhdev, leader of the UN Environment Programme's Economics of Ecosystems and Biodiversity study, called Singapore "a model that most urban centres should emulate".[26]

The Garden City brand positioning has also been reinforced by all the branding around a special orchid as Singapore's national flower – the hybrid called Vanda Miss Joaquim, renamed Papilionanthe Miss Joaquim in 2011 after further research showed that this orchid actually belongs to the Papilionanthe genus. The remarkable propensity of the orchid to sprout new hybrid subspecies has allowed for a unique nation branding platform by way of having hybrids named after international public figures and celebrities. The first VIP orchid here was the Aranthera Anne Black, named after the wife of the then governor of Singapore, Sir Robert Black, in 1956. Since then, Singapore has named more than 200 VIP orchid hybrids for visiting heads of state – such as Queen Elizabeth II, Jordan's King Abdullah II, Myanmar's Premier Thein Sein – and celebrities such as Italian singer Andrea Bocelli, Indian actor Amitabh Bachchan and South Korean actor Bae Yong Jun. These named hybrids are placed in a VIP Orchid Garden in the National Orchid Garden, located within the Singapore Botanic Gardens.

Going forward, just as one would prune and fertilise an orchid plant with care, the management of this branding channel can be further refined for more careful propagation and promotion, so as to plant even more fertile seeds, and perhaps to reap a more bountiful harvest of positive gain for nation branding. A great platform for doing this was secured when the Singapore Botanic Gardens was named as the country's first UNESCO World Heritage Site in 2015 at a ceremony in Bonn, Germany. It is only the world's third botanic gardens to be listed as a World Heritage Site, after Kew Gardens in England and Padua Gardens in Italy. Being realised in the "SG50" year, the Gardens' UNESCO inscription was like a bonus to add to the golden jubilee celebrations. The UNESCO inscription was the fruit of five years' work from 2010, when Singapore conducted a feasibility study on the possible sites to be put up for inscription, with the earlier contenders including Little India, Chinatown and Fort Canning. These other sites might hold promise of more such inscriptions in future.

The paradigm shift:
"City in a Garden" to "City in Nature"

From the early 2000s, the "Garden City" moved into a new phase of reinvention. The new approach was captured in the term "City in a Garden" – a clever inversion of the term "Garden City" that transformed its meaning totally. This vision has been described by Ngiam Tong Dow, former permanent secretary for national development, in superlative terms: "I do not think that even Babylon, with its legendary hanging gardens, can be conceived of as the city garden that Singapore aspires to be."[27] Mr Ngiam was referring to the concept of the former head of the National Parks Board (NParks), Dr Kiat W. Tan, of turning Singapore from a garden city (or city of gardens) into a city set in a garden. In a garden city, land and space are selectively set aside and developed into gardens and parks, such as the world-renowned Singapore Botanic Gardens, in essence creating green oases here and there within the city. But setting a city within a garden goes into an entirely new, much more holistic, dimension altogether. As Mr Ngiam said: "By considering the whole of Singapore as one beautiful garden, the possibilities for NParks to exercise their imagination and creativity soared. With this paradigm shift came ambitious plans such as linking all the major parks in Singapore with a network of cycling tracks, and developing Singapore as 'the first city garden in the world'."

A prominent launch pad for projecting nation branding along this theme internationally is now provided by Gardens by the Bay, a set of three public gardens on Marina Bay right on the waterfront.[28] The main garden, Gardens at Bay South, was completed in 2011. The project has been hailed as being symbolic of Singapore's major differentiating factor as a city-state in integrating greenery and gardens into far-sighted and coordinated city planning and the enhancement of quality of life, in the process putting other Asian cities such as Hong Kong, Seoul and Taipei in the shade, figuratively and literally.[29] Being seen as leading in greening is a precious resource in today's world beset by serious concerns of environmental degradation, rapid urbanisation and the damaging effects of climate change.

Only in an ideal world would there be no opposition to a branding proposition. And Gardens by the Bay is no exception. For instance, the Nature Society of Singapore, a civil society organisation advocating care for nature, wrote a report stating that while it welcomed the creation of the gardens, more could be done to make the area look more natural. The main criticism was that "it looks more or less like a theme park",[30] as if theme parks were inherently bad. To address this line of thinking, in the branding effort of Gardens by the Bay, one approach might be not to try to win this ideological tussle through confrontation but to amplify the pluses that the Gardens can bring. These initial doubting voices have all but subsided, and today, only nature-loving purists have anything negative to say about the Gardens.

There can be no doubt that Gardens by the Bay – with attractions such as glass-domed conservatories with controlled climatic conditions, and concrete vertical planting structures called "Supertrees" – will put Singapore prominently on the world map of places of exceptional botanical interest. Having something in the same league as other botanically themed attractions such as the Eden Project in Cornwall in Britain, and possibly even surpassing them in some ways, will add substantially to nation branding for Singapore.

At the individual level, Singapore's "City in a Garden" branding will be absorbed and internalised through a very personal and memorable experience of this brand journey. For a visitor to Singapore, flying in to the tropical island (preferably on a Singapore Airlines flight), the first impression of the place is framed and fostered by the tree- and shrub-lined East Coast Parkway leading in to the city, with the shoreline and sea to the southern side just off the highway. This experience – with all the power of a first impression – has enhanced Singapore's nation branding in the minds and hearts of many visitors, consciously or subconsciously, since the opening of Changi Airport in 1981.

And now, as is typical of Singapore, it gets even better. This physical and psychological entry "avenue" to the country is being enhanced with developments at Marina Bay around the new business and financial centre, especially Gardens by the Bay. Approaching the city along a curved highway, and looking across the Marina Channel right after passing the Singapore Flyer, the stunning domes of the two glass conservatories and Supertrees of Gardens by the Bay will appear to rise up to greet the viewer. Whereas the Eden Project is more than a day trip from London away in the countryside, Singapore's Gardens by the Bay is right in the city centre, at the mouth of the Singapore River. Physically and spiritually, Gardens by the Bay and the "City in a Garden" vision are right at the heart of the new Singapore.

This brand positioning is enhanced by an accompanying event also aspiring towards world-class standards – the Singapore Garden Festival. Held every other year since 2006 and growing from strength to strength, this international garden and flower show brings more top garden designers from more countries together than any other show, including Britain's famed Chelsea Flower Show.

That Singapore chose to put down roots – and so deeply – into this strand of nation branding of gardens and greenery so many years ago, and the way it is now taking this initiative to a whole new level, will stand the country in very good stead for the future. Nature-loving purists in large countries with mountain ranges and rolling meadows may scoff, but what Singapore has achieved is to make the best of very limited natural resources. To nurture co-existence with nature amidst quality high-density living requires the clever use of "artifice", as with the artificial Supertrees for solar power generation and display of 158,000 plants of more than 700 species at Gardens by the Bay. The artifice of human intervention has also helped boost biodiversity across the rest of the island. For example, the Oriental pied hornbill, which vanished from the island in the 19th century and returned only in the 1990s, now flourishes in the hundreds. By installing man-made wooden nest boxes in trees for these birds to breed in, the Singapore Hornbill Project's collaborators (including NParks, Wildlife Reserves Singapore and researchers) helped to attract visiting birds from neighbouring countries to settle here and raise their young.[31]

As the world becomes even more concerned about combating climate change, alongside managing the tipping point in global rural-urban migration, Singapore's green nation branding should enable it to stand out all the more. Going forward, Singapore's national greenery project is evolving once more, this time to nurture a "City in Nature". The "City in a Garden" will mature even further to restore nature into the urban fabric and enhance ecological connectivity and biodiversity. One initiative is for NParks to continue to expand the Park Connector Network to enable every household eventually to be within a 10-minute walk from a park. Concrete canals are being converted back to streams lined by grassy slopes, adorned with flowering plants. Another movement is for the community to be galvanised to help plant a million trees across Singapore over 10 years.

This latest "City in Nature" phase in Singapore's development of its greenery is going full circle, like travelling back in time. It is a return – as far as is possible amidst such intensive high-rise urbanisation – to a natural environment that will thrive in enough pockets and stretches across the terrain, as to bring the splendour and sustenance of nature to all residents on this island.[32]

The mastery of man

On another level, Gardens by the Bay exemplifies a vital overall brand attribute of Singapore – the application of human ingenuity to overcome constraints of nature, so as to enhance the quality of life. In this, the element of artifice inherent as in a theme park is precisely what is needed to create greater benefits that would otherwise not exist, for example, generating awareness of conservation and climate change by bringing to this international tourism hub on the Equator a slice of the flora of Mediterranean, montane and other climates.

In the same way, it was quite an innovation and a very smart move in brand differentiation and positioning for such a small and urbanised place to have the world's first Night Safari. The park, with over 900 animals of 100 species (more than a third of them endangered), attracts over 1.3 million visitors annually.[33] The basic idea itself for the park is as fetching as it is far-sighted and simple – to display animals at their most active in nocturnal activity. Animals, after all, are mostly naturally nocturnal, so generally zoos have, in a sense, "got it wrong" all along, catering more to the body clock of humans than that of animals.

The theme of the mastery of human intervention is also at the root of another aspect of Singapore's overriding international image – that of a city where everything works, trains always run on time, and the lights (almost) never go out. These brand attributes have been realised through the hard work of many agencies over the years. That the lights always work is the fruit of the labour of the Energy Market Authority and, before 2001, the Public Utilities Board. The PUB, in turn, with all its efforts in sourcing for alternative ways to produce clean drinking water – including desalination, reverse osmosis, and water-recycling to create "NEWater" – has moved the nation practically into self-sufficiency in water, after decades of having to rely on imported water and hence feeling much national anxiety and vulnerability. Singapore is now even in a strong position to export its expertise to help other countries enhance their access to clean water. In addition to ensuring an adequate and secure supply of utilities, there is an overall strategic eye on the future that leaves no stone unturned in considering all options, including the feasibility of nuclear energy for the long term, which Singapore has embarked on studying.[34]

Singapore's physical infrastructure has many other projects in the pipeline that will transform the island even further in many forms in future, including the Greater Southern

Waterfront to redevelop a wide stretch of real estate on the southern coast, the world's first fully automated port terminal at Tuas Mega Port, Jurong Lake District for a decentralised development "from boondocks to boom town" in the west, Jurong Rock Cavern for underground industrial storage and other subterranean uses, and Punggol Digital District to testbed smart city solutions. Such ambitious infrastructure projects are possible only because of a unique brand attribute of Singapore – its capacity for its urban planners, architects and engineers to operate as "urban systems innovators",[35] always seeking new solutions to provide everything from potable drinking water to uninterrupted Wi-Fi. Taking a systems approach to plan ahead holistically to cover all relevant aspects, these innovators are always able to plan for the entire country because of the state's high level of land ownership, and for the long-term because of political stability. At the same time, in the private sector, outstanding projects continue to transform Singapore's skyline and earn international recognition. For example, the luxury condominium Reflections at Keppel Bay, designed by Daniel Liebeskind, was the setting as a futuristic habitat in the 2015 Hollywood science-fiction movie *Equals,* together with other locations such as Marina Barrage and Henderson Waves.

On top of this is the political will to commit and invest significant resources to priority areas, such as what some consider the greatest challenge to mankind – tackling climate change. The national Budget of February 2020 included an announcement of a S$100 billion (about US$72 billion) plan to safeguard the city against temperatures and floodwaters several times the levels of the Paris agreement – keeping the global temperature increase to about 1.5 degrees Celsius and the rise in sea levels to less than 0.5 metres.[36] The options for the government are expected to be varied, from using mangrove to protect coastlines to flood-proofing subway stations and developing green "sponge" areas to absorb floodwaters. Another stated target in this "car-lite society" is to phase out private vehicles with internal combustion engines and to replace them completely with electric cars by 2040. Singapore also aims to become a circular economy and zero-waste nation, a move accelerated by Covid-19. Food sustainability will be boosted by initiatives such as promoting sea-based farming. Launched at a time when governments around the world are struggling to meet such goals, Singapore's sustainability plans deserve to be better-known, to encourage other nations to also chip in for the sake of the survival of humanity on this planet.

Overall, an absolutely reliable total infrastructure for business and investment is the foundation for thematic taglines that have been conceived and presented at major nation branding platforms, such as "Global City, World of Opportunities" at the World Bank/International Monetary Fund meetings hosted by Singapore in 2006. While this event was mainly for finance ministers and officials and other attendees from the world of finance and financial services, it sought to brand Singapore as a whole for all industry sectors. This was also the case when Singapore hosted the Asia-Pacific Economic Cooperation (Apec) Economic Leaders Meeting in November 2009, which saw nation branding efforts extend far beyond trade, such as in a video titled "Singapore: Where the world meets".[37] For these events, Singapore was practising one of the most elemental principles of branding: Doing well is great, but to do really well, it is necessary to let the right people know that you're doing really well.

Letting more people know you're doing well was also a leading intention behind Singapore's hosting of the North Korea–United States Singapore Summit meeting between North Korean Chairman Kim Jong-un and US President Donald Trump, held on Sentosa in June 2018. The talks were positioned as a major step towards the eventual denuclearisation of the Korean peninsula, but later, the negotiations fell apart and scuttled this possibility. The Singapore government saw a landmark nation branding opportunity, as the event would build on the city-state's branding as the "Switzerland of Asia".[38]

This highly positive nickname had been given to Singapore as far back as the 1970s,[39] when it referred more to the then-still very young republic's status as a global financial centre in Asia, modelled after the best Swiss practices of handling and holding money. In 2018, the reference was more to Singapore's reputed public safety and neutrality in foreign relations. Navigating safe passage amongst the globe's big powers, and skilfully maintaining friendly relations, with enlightened national interest, remains a key feature of Singapore's high standing in the world, all the more so in a post-Covid-19 world.

Singapore as a "global entrepolis"

In recent years, another dimension of branding Singapore on the basis of human ingenuity has been advanced through the global positioning of the technology precinct called Fusionopolis, founded on the groundbreaking notion of multiple disciplines of science and technology coming together in one location to integrate knowledge and create new value for the global economy. The complex, together with the neighbouring research hub Biopolis housing research and industry players in the life sciences, as well as the adjacent Mediapolis for media and information technology, is part of a larger area built with the same vision. Called "one-north", the area was designed by the renowned architect and urban planner Zaha Hadid. This home to research and entrepreneurship has been called "an entire integrated innovation ecosystem".[40]

Fusionopolis and the rest of one-north is a microcosm of what Singapore itself stands for as a nation – state-led initiatives creating a conducive environment for new ideas in engineering and the hard sciences to flourish, so as to produce new engines of growth for the economy. The advocacy for truly multi-disciplinary integration of knowledge is also espoused by educational institutions such as the Singapore University of Technology and Design, set up in collaboration with the Massachusetts Institute of Technology. Embedded in these initiatives is an idea that is daring in its potential for brand differentiation – to overcome the human tendency for "silo thinking", that is, thinking and behaving primarily according to one's own narrow area of interest and perspective of the world.

There have also been other umbrella branding initiatives over the years that have spoken directly to audience segments from clusters of sectors of the world economy. Agencies such as the Economic Development Board have used various concepts and buzzwords to promote Singapore as a place to set up factories and regional offices in growth industry sectors. One of these branding concepts and visions of the future is the idea of Singapore as yet another kind of "polis" (or city) – a "global entrepolis". The term was coined by the EDB in 2003 from putting together "polis" and three Es – entrepot, enterprise and entrepreneurship – representing the three main phases of Singapore's evolution as a business centre, from a strategic trading post since the days of the ancient maritime Silk Route, to a desired home for multinational companies, to a magnet for startups and hot money from all across the globe.[41]

The concept of a "global entrepolis" encapsulates a few of Singapore's unique value propositions. Singapore is one of the world's only three city-states – together with Monaco and the Vatican City – and the only one that is also a sovereign state. This is special because, since Singapore is also a country, it is a city that has everything that an investor might want, from protection of intellectual property to the best supply chain management. In larger countries, it would not be politically acceptable to position everything into one location, so, in the US, for example, finance is centred in New York while technology is clustered all the way on the opposite coast in Silicon Valley. In Singapore, every business need is available via face-to-face meetings with the right partners drawn from the world's best, who are all less than an hour's drive away. What's more, national will and resources can be marshalled to back any business initiative, and policies can be adjusted much faster, and with a lot more certainty, than in other political systems and business cultures. The "global entrepolis" idea became an international event, Global Entrepolis@Singapore, drawing businessmen, investors and supporting industry players to meet in Singapore and seek new business opportunities.

Expertise for export and generating "buzz"

Singapore has done so well with its own economic development programmes that it has taken this expertise to the regional and global arena – in a sense moving from the GDP world to that of GNP (gross national product). This would never have happened had it not been for a foundation of effective nation branding. Over the years, the republic has offered advice and consultancy to other governments in areas such as the building of industrial estates and urban planning. In China, for example, government-to-government collaboration has left a mark in the development of places such as Suzhou with its industrial parks, and has in recent years also begun to create a legacy in other projects such as Tianjin Eco-city and Guangzhou Knowledge City, based on collaborative agreements between the governments of China and Singapore to incorporate newer elements such as sustainable aspects of development.

More recently, such expertise continues to find new export avenues. One example is the agency called Singapore Cooperation Enterprise (SCE), formed by the Ministry of Trade and Industry and the Ministry of Foreign Affairs, to respond to the many foreign requests to tap Singapore's development experience. SCE works closely with Singapore's government ministries and statutory boards to tailor solutions to match the foreign parties' needs. Such programmes could include visits, training, advisory services and project implementation. SCE also invites participation from relevant private sector players, including representatives from trade and industry associations. Project clients come from as far away as Tanzania.

One element of branding success is the extent to which a brand is able to create new market segments even as it consolidates its appeal to existing segments. On this score,

Singapore has benefited from government-led efforts to penetrate fresh markets in new parts of the world such as the whole Middle East region,[42] including fast-growing markets like Kuwait and the United Arab Emirates, Singapore's largest and most mature market in the Middle East.

Meanwhile, the strong growth in visitor arrivals is part of the burgeoning interest internationally in visiting Singapore, with the opening of two multi-billion-dollar integrated resorts which have been seen as key drivers in Singapore's transformation as a destination for leisure as well as for business. Resorts World Sentosa has Southeast Asia's first Universal Studios, featuring rides including the world's only *Madagascar* attraction. The other integrated resort, Marina Bay Sands, includes an ArtScience museum and a Skypark 57 storeys high, featuring the world's largest outdoor infinity swimming pool, offering a spectacular view of the city.

The two integrated resorts have already – and will always, from now on – contribute to nation branding for Singapore, in the way that they permanently alter the skyline. The reversal in the government policy position on casinos that enabled the two integrated resorts to be built also changed the nation branding game for Singapore in significant ways. Siting the Sands casino in the historic civic centre and central business district could not be more "in-your-face" in a way that challenges – and forever transforms – any attempt by foreign observers to straitjacket Singapore to its old image in the Western media of being stiff, stuffy and sterile.

Brand Singapore

The city's "buzz" – another word much-favoured by Singapore's civil servants in economic agencies – is also being taken to new heights by private-sector developments such as the enduring success of the dance club Zouk and its outdoor dance music festival Zoukout, which celebrated its 15th anniversary in 2015. The fact that Southeast Asia's largest beach party is held in the region's tiniest country says a lot about Singapore's brand ambitions and achievements.

The boldness of such moves to jazz up nocturnal excitement in the Lion City – and the scale on which they have been mounted – would not have been possible without the approval and all-out backing of the government. A much less often observed fact about Zoukout is that it is Singapore's reputation for public safety that enables the smooth organisation of such a large-scale event, drawing thousands of scantily clad and inebriated young people and the young-at-heart. The nation branding effect of such hip events on potential audiences out there is still being formed, and is worthy of deeper study. The question now is surely not how stuffy or sterile Singapore is, but how much less so it has become and is becoming. Singapore used to be disparagingly called "Disneyland with the death penalty".[43] In a manner of speaking, the death penalty may still be around, and there is no Disneyland yet, but what a new "Universal Studios effect" there is now.

Formula One: Turning night into day

Most of the initiatives to inject more "vibrancy" into Singapore have one eye on the attraction of foreign talent. This includes augmenting the labour force with knowhow, skills and networks from abroad, as well as more targeted efforts to attract quality immigrants. In recent years, this has gained urgency and more concerted effort, given Singapore's steadily declining fertility rate, which has fallen below the replacement level of 2.1 since 1975, and hit a record low of 1.14 in 2019. The quality of life in Singapore that government agencies toil tirelessly to enhance has, as it were, moved systematically up Maslow's hierarchy of needs through the decades, from the basic physiological needs in the 1960s like drinking water (tackled with NEWater and desalination) to self-actualisation today through arts and entertainment activities such as touring the National Gallery or attending a Formula One race.

In the wake of the Remaking Singapore committee of 2002, whose task was to propose a social and political makeover for the republic for the 21st century, as well as other review committees since then, including the Committee on the Future Economy formed in 2015, more and more sacred cows have been put to the sword of revamp, mainly for the sake of boosting the GDP but also for talent attraction. Singapore is actually pretty good at proffering paradigm shifts. One of the most illuminating in recent years has been the establishment of the Formula One Grand Prix night race in Singapore. Since the first race in 2008, the event has become a much-anticipated fixture on the international racing calendar. The power of projecting to TV and online audiences worldwide Singapore's spectacular skyline – highlighted by the new Marina Bay Sands integrated resort and framed on the other side by British colonial buildings such as the former City Hall and Supreme Court, and Victoria Theatre and Concert Hall – should not be underestimated. One visitor, Craig Arnott, who travelled from his home in Gloucester, England to attend the 2010 race, told the Singapore media: "When I saw the backdrop on television last year, I told my kids that we've got to see it in person. Now that we're here, it really looks like one giant postcard."[44] To have this kind of magnetic effect, and be on people's "bucket list" of must-visit places, is a prime example of the power of nation branding. This kind of brand equity can survive even any disruption thrown up by a pandemic.

Formula One is a particularly attractive branding platform in that, unlike other sporting events, it is one of the very few that happen practically all year round and all over the world. Formula One power broker Bernie Ecclestone has said he would like Singapore to continue hosting the night race for the next 20 years, calling the Singapore race the sport's "crown jewel".[45] The event's nation branding potential is set to grow into the rest of Asia as well, given the sport's expansion into the world's fastest-growing continent. The creation of Formula One's first night race in Singapore was nothing short of groundbreaking in nation branding terms.

Moreover, by changing the very nature of the event – turning night into day (with the street lighting) and day into night (getting the drivers and crews to adapt to the unusual timing of this leg of the race) – the Singapore event adroitly negated the "accreditation effect"[46] usually associated with hosting globally familiar events such as Formula One. The danger was that hosting the event could have made the republic more like other Formula One locations rather than different from them. This similarity with other cities would have reduced any nation branding benefit. But by the time the inaugural race was over, however, that worry had been quashed incontrovertibly. The Formula One race 2020 might have been cancelled in view of the Covid-19 restrictions on travel and events, but, in any event, Singapore's position as the pioneer host of the world's first Formula One race to be held after the sun has set can never be taken away. As they say, you always remember the first time. No one remembers who came in second.

In a similar way, securing the bid to host the inaugural Youth Olympic Games in August 2010 was another coup in Singapore's nation branding. The YOG, featuring 3,500 young athletes from around the world, were the first new Games launched by the International Olympic Committee since the Winter Games of 1924. The opening and closing ceremony shows, directed by Singapore theatre director Ivan

Heng, were beamed to millions in 72 countries. The anniversary of these Singapore Games is now marked every year by the YOG, held annually ever since. The memorial Youth Olympic Park at Singapore's Marina Bay waterfront continues to inspire young sportsmen.

LKY and after

On the topic of the government's role in nation branding, one cannot miss out mention of the tremendous part played by major political authority figures, chief among them Lee Kuan Yew, who was prime minister from 1959 to 1990 and thereafter held the post of Senior Minister and then Minister Mentor in the Singapore Cabinet until the general election in May 2011. Even after his death in March 2015, his influence over brand Singapore endures, although this will naturally diminish as more time passes, as some observers have already noted, as is the case with other world leaders such as China's Mao Zedong.

Most of the Singapore public sector initiatives discussed in this chapter have been credited to Mr Lee, either as his brainchild (such as the Garden City vision) or only executed with his "blessings" (such as the U-turn on casinos). When he was still politically active, hardly a day would go by without his being cited in the international media, usually on the subject of governance and international relations, when the subtext was really nation branding, even if no one overtly mentioned the term or even consciously intended it. As an individual, he had more mentions in media platforms that influence global opinion about Singapore than any other Singaporean, or anyone else for that matter. Everything he said or did had an impact on nation branding. With his memoirs now being made available to more and more audiences internationally,[47] the reach of his values and beliefs continues to stretch by the day. Among politicians, senior civil servants and scholars and students of politics, his contribution to nation branding is undeniable, and his fans are decidedly numerous, thousands of whom gathered to mourn his passing in 2015. In the standard branding word-association test – the ultimate yardstick – the moment that "Singapore" is mentioned, many people think of "Lee Kuan Yew".

Indeed, one could even say that Mr Lee's contribution to nation branding is quantifiable to some extent, although adding up all the numbers would be some task – not only because of the wide span of direct and indirect impact, but also because he had been at it since the 1960s. Chan Chin Bock, former chairman of EDB, recalled how in the 1960s and 70s, Mr Lee, when he was prime minister, would almost never miss meeting the EDB's potential client companies during his trips to the USA. The eloquent politician's most vital value-add in these investment promotion situations was to "explain the political outlook on Southeast Asian countries to nervous investors".[48] Mr Lee continued to play this role even into his 80s, and was routinely looked up to as that rare elder statesman of Asia who always had incisive insights to offer to political and economic players and observers.

Speaking at the Global Brand Forum 2004 event in Singapore, Mr Lee revealed that it was only in hindsight that he and the Singapore government realised that the concerted move to set Singapore apart from other nations over the years was an exercise in nation branding. In the past, he confessed, "I did not know the word 'brand' at all."[49] The key to nation branding was that, besides establishing a reputation for having an honest and efficient government, the island-state also emphasised integrity at all levels of its civil administration, to maintain its credibility. The example he cited was the SARS crisis of 2003, when the Singapore government was forthcoming in acknowledging the severity of the emerging viral epidemic. The government's tough stance on SARS, he said, set Singapore's economy back considerably, but in the long run, "established Singapore as different". How the Singapore government will be assessed to have managed the Covid-19 pandemic, after it finally subsides, will certainly also shape the future standing of the country brand.

Despite Singapore's success in building its reputation over the years, Mr Lee warned the nation against being complacent and losing its competitive edge. "Being number one does not mean we will be number one next year," he added. The country's key to remaining competitive would be to stay relevant to its partner nations by always being able to add value to them, since "it is a never-ending battle to keep your position". Indeed, the game of nation branding requires unending vigilance, somewhat like the way that Singapore's approach to working for its success has been likened to cycling on a tightrope, where the pedalling must never stop. Mr Lee applied this mentality to the way he took care to prepare and perform well for every nation branding platform, whether it was as a keynote speaker to an audience of thousands at a global forum or to just one person at an in-depth interview on an influential international media platform.

Fuller assessments about the whole range of Mr Lee's contributions to nation branding, however, will be realised only in the future. His name was mentioned a few times in the runup to the 2020 general election, mostly to connect a politician's current statement with a longstanding political belief. But clearly, the immediate impact and appeal that his words commanded when he was alive had already diminished with the passing of time, as is the case with all, even the strongest, leaders in history.

Also, Mr Lee's legacy has been somewhat complicated by what came to be known as the "Oxley Road saga". In 2017, Mr Lee's home at 38 Oxley Road became central to a dispute among his children – Prime Minister Lee Hsien Loong, Lee Hsien Yang and Dr Lee Wei Ling – over its future use and possible demolition. Mr Lee Hsien Yang joined the opposition Progress Singapore Party and helped to campaign at GE2020. During the hustings, one of his main comments to the media was that the PAP of his father's time "had lost its way".[50]

In recent years, more members of the "Old Guard" of first-generation Cabinet ministers have passed on – including former culture minister S. Rajaratnam, and former defence minister Goh Keng Swee. The biographies about them are adding to that pool of additional perspectives on Singapore's equivalent of a nation's founding myths. Key ideas and sentiments from these pioneers will be presented in the Founders' Memorial when it is built in the coming years. These and other materials will add to the resources that audiences outside Singapore and Singaporeans themselves can draw upon to assess the brand essence infused into the spirit of the Singapore people at all levels, judging by the lives and legacies of those who have exercised leadership at the highest levels of government, as well as those they have governed.

The reserved Presidency:
Symbol to the world

In 2016, Singapore's Constitution was amended to introduce a "hiatus-triggered model" to ensure that the elected Presidency would be reserved for candidates from the minority groups of Malay Singaporeans, and of Indian, Eurasian or other ethnicities, if members of either of these two groups had not held the Presidency for five terms. This was a daring political move by the ruling People's Action Party, which holds the potential for deep influence on brand Singapore hereafter.

The financial requirements of eligibility for the elected Presidency were also raised for candidates from the private sector. Halimah Yacob, a veteran Member of Parliament of the PAP, turned out to be the only qualified candidate, based on her previous Speaker of Parliament role, and was elected unopposed in 2017. She became the first female President, and the second Muslim since Yusof Ishak, in the country's history. She is also Southeast Asia's fourth female head of state after Corazon Aquino and Gloria Macapagal Arroyo of the Philippines and Megawati Sukarnoputri of Indonesia.

President Halimah's walkover election drew considerable concern among Singaporeans over its process, and the PAP even conceded that there might be a political price to pay for making this debatable Constitutional change.[51] But outside of Singapore, having her as head of state has had, and will most likely continue to have, significant impact on how people around the world perceive Singapore, in a world that has viewed any aspect of Islamic culture through different lenses ever since the 911 attacks in the USA in 2001. In addition to the aspect of race and religion, observers are also taking note of the President's gender, minority status and humble socio-economic beginnings in life.

Externally, reactions from the region, and further afield, have been overwhelmingly positive, for example, as expressed in a congratulatory statement by a Malaysian MP from the Islamic party Amana, Dr Siti Mariah Mahmud, that Singapore's new President is "an iconic image that emphasises harmony and stability… as the world is still struggling with regressive issues regarding women and Islamophobia".[52] The irony here is that the "fine city" of seemingly rigid rules and regulations is, in some ways, more fluid, welcoming and conducive than many other nations in the inflow and upward mobility of people and ideas, as it has always been in goods and services. The symbolic power of this Presidency reaffirms, and fleshes out, the vital brand attribute of social cohesiveness, validated by Singapore's status as the most religiously diverse country in the world, as recognised in a 2014 Pew Research Center study of the religious makeup of more than 200 countries and territories.[53] This has become an even more precious brand attribute amidst the heightened race consciousness and other divides that have surfaced among people across the world in the second half of the 2010s.

As for the internal dimension of brand Singapore, clearly, the power of the Presidency as a symbol and role model for multiculturalism and minority representation – and also, more contentiously, for meritocracy – was appreciated and intended by the ruling party. This was captured in the words of Prime Minister Lee Hsien Loong at the swearing-in, that the new President represents "who we are and what we want to be" as a society and nation.[54] Among the selfie-hunting crowds who rush forward at the new President's public appearances will be young Singaporeans who, growing up with an authority figure like her, must surely be positively influenced – at least in some way, and if only subconsciously – in their own sense of multiracialism and social mobility.

Overall, then, any allusion to the "Passion Made Possible" brand concept was never intended, but there *is* a connection between Halimah's Presidency and the new country brand's aim to showcase the attributes of the typical Singaporean's earnestness, energy and enterprising spirit. When it comes to branding, coherence is always useful. And here is an unplanned aspect of symbolic symmetry: Singapore's President – once an ordinary woman, now head of state – is herself an emblem of passion made possible.[55]

Singapore's Bicentennial: History revised, reaffirmed

The year 2019 was devoted to commemorating 200 years since 1819, when Thomas Stamford Raffles arrived with the East India Company in Singapore and started the process of claiming the island for the British Crown. As part of this year of reflection, the "binoculars" of historical perspective were also turned backwards to look into 700 years of ancient history dating back to Sang Nila Utama, a Srivijayan prince from Palembang (in what is today Indonesia) who was the founder of the Kingdom of Singapura in 1299, with a rich history in the intervening centuries.

From the 13th to 14th century, Singapore was called Temasek, a name recorded in Chinese sources as Dan Ma Xi.

The island was alternately claimed by the Siamese and Javanese, and changed its name to Singapura perhaps towards
the end of the 14th century. Singapura was controlled by the
Sultanate of Malacca in the 15th century and the Sultanate
of Johor as a trading centre from the 16th century. In 1613,
Portuguese raiders burnt down the settlement at the mouth
of the Singapore River and the island sank into obscurity,
until the British arrived.

To mark the 2019 Bicentennial, the Singapore government curated a year-long nationwide series of activities, with
extensive community outreach to, and engagement with,
partners including associations, clans and religious and cultural organisations, prompting them to do their own historical reassessments. This was a significant exercise in fostering
social and political cohesion, which was not without its risks,
in terms of arousing inspiration for deeper research into the
past that might not be totally congruent with the official narrative of more recent periods of history.

The year-long effort in public education also carried the
potential for deep impact in internal country brand-building, some of which was bolstered by external validation. For
example, *Becoming Singapore*, a made-for-TV documentary
revolving around a search into her Eurasian family history
by former Nominated Member of Parliament Eunice Olsen,
won a bronze award at the New York Festivals TV & Film
Awards. At home, one takeaway from this show is the reflection that, hitherto, many Singaporeans had comparatively

little interest in genealogy, perhaps because of a lack of self-confidence among formerly colonised peoples, in contrast to the often-swelling pride in ancestry felt by citizens of imperial nations.[55] Such a reawakened awareness of identity and belonging may be an ingredient into the brand attribute of a strong sense of self-determination. But it could also spur a fresh reckoning by ordinary people on their relationship with power, that might, in turn, challenge the very basis of that self-determined vision of the future

The Bicentennial programme started with a bang. At the start of the year, four new full-sized statues – of Sang Nila Utama, Raffles' scribe Munshi Abdullah and community philanthropists Tan Tock Seng and Naraina Pillai – were placed overnight surrounding the statue of Raffles that was erected in 1972 by the Singapore River. At first, some observers thought that Raffles' hitherto pre-eminent position in history might finally be dislodged, and imperialism put in its proper place as a problematic period of history. However, such post-colonial "hopes" could not be further off the mark. After one week, the four new statues were moved away to less prominent locations further along the river promenade, restoring Raffles to his unchallenged pride of place. After a year, they were removed completely, erasing visible memory of the Bicentennial exercise.

More importantly, what unfolded the rest of the year was that Raffles was, in fact, being placed on a new pedestal by this commemoration. His tenure in Singapore's history was clearly more freehold than leasehold, his mythical role perpetuated as a "subliminal beacon"[57] to welcome trade, investment and immigration to these shores. The new "monument" to Raffles was not figurative but concrete, including the unveiling of Raffles House, refurbished from an original bungalow built in 1822 where Raffles had stayed, surveying the port from the summit of Fort Canning Hill. This is one of nine gardens renovated or built by the National Parks Board to mark the Bicentennial. Another monument in the private sector also reopened that year – the refurbished Raffles Hotel, which has resumed serving Singapore Slings once again.

Clearly, two centuries later, there is still essentially no change to how Raffles is being viewed officially in Singapore, from 1960, when the Dutch economist Albert Winsemius first arrived as a United Nations development expert. As revealed in the book *Seven Hundred Years: A History of Singapore*: "Singapore's leaders internalised the Dutchman's advice about the practicality of prominently displaying Raffles' statue as a subliminal marker of a young nation's trustworthiness and credibility to becalm and attract modern, wealthy, largely Western investor nations."[58] The use of the archaic verb "becalm" here underscores the value of the symbolism of Raffles, which looks set to continue to be a key success factor for this global city's economic growth and social harmony.

Singapore's unorthodox way of leveraging its colonial past for economic branding benefit is sustainable only because, on subjects as important as the dominant perspective on its political history, the official narrative is managed in a more sophisticated way than by some other countries. Alternative narratives are not crushed but allowed to surface, so long as they lack the traction and critical mass to change the average person's worldview. For example, the play *Merdeka*, staged that year by the theatre company Wild Rice, asked important questions about problematic episodes of history such as the 1954 Chinese high school riots against the colonial government's attempt to introduce national service, and what really happened to the Malay merchant Syed Yassin who stabbed British Resident William Farquhar. Even as the official narrative sustains its dominance, such stories of ordinary folks from colonial times actually deserve more attention, to give a fuller sense of Singapore's past and shape a more inclusive shared path towards the future.

But what people will remember instead, even if only subliminally, are the official key takeaways from the year's main event – *The Bicentennial Experience*, a multimedia exhibition at Fort Canning Park presenting seven centuries of history with live actors, digital media and other materials, that drew a total visitorship exceeding nine million. This show is noteworthy in terms of highlighting three national brand attributes "embedded in the Singaporean DNA" – openness, multiculturalism and self-determination – which had evolved through history and were positioned as vital to facing the challenges today, and charting the future. After viewing the exhibition, audiences were asked to vote which attribute resonated most with them. Self-determination, the most "political" of the three, was the crowd favourite.

The government's "visible hand"

In its state-led nation branding initiatives, Singapore proves some branding theorists wrong. There are two main weaknesses often observed of nation branding compared with corporate branding. One is that usually "there's nobody in charge", and the other is that branding efforts have short timeframes because of changes in political leadership, usually when a political party loses power in a general election, or when the politician in charge of nation branding is changed for political or other reasons.[59] On both counts, Singapore is atypical – there *is* someone fully in charge (although brand-building happens more at the sub-brand level than completely controlled centrally with a holistic overview), and that someone (the ruling party) has been around for more than 50 years; hence, the timeframes for nation branding initiatives in Singapore are longer than in most nations.

Yet, while the timeframes for branding projects are not shorter for political reasons, they are sometimes shorter than they should be for other reasons, including changes in top public-sector executive appointments in agencies involved in nation branding efforts. This last factor is usually part of the job-rotation and talent-grooming process in the political system and bureaucracy. In general, strategic policy directions in Singapore change remarkably little with Cabinet reshuffles, because the personality of the politician in charge is much less of a factor in Singapore's political system, in which strategic policy directions – including for nation branding – are set and sustained over a much longer timeframe. Nonetheless, at a more tactical level for senior government officials, sometimes branding decisions are made on the wrong basis, to satisfy short-term KPIs (key performance indicators) or just to "score points" and be different from the previous person in charge.

The role of government agencies in conceptualising and directing nation branding efforts is part of the broader manifestation of the "visible hand" of the state in all public affairs. This is a corollary to the 18th-century Scottish economist and moral philosopher Adam Smith's concept of the "invisible hand"[60] that directs the free market (with its basic underlying profit motive) to achieve economic outcomes that eventually turn out to be for the general good. Here, the similarity between invisible and visible hands is perhaps instructive to further enhance the overriding operating mechanism in the advancement of nation branding.

The invisible hand of free markets has a self-regulating principle, and this impetus should be allowed to reach for fuller expression also in the case of the visible hand in nation branding. For instance, an ideal free market requires complete information. Of course, total information is a theoretical ideal, but the key operating principle should be that more information is always better than less. Hence, new information such as feedback on a branding concept should not be ignored or overruled in favour of an alternative idea judged, say, on the rank of its proposer rather than the idea's inherent quality, as is wont to happen especially in a rank-conscious system.

Another important point is that new initiatives should be launched only after deep enough analysis of previous efforts, and of changes in the global and sectoral environment. But this process is often shortened, because of the same systemic weaknesses of too-frequent job rotations and focusing too much on KPIs, not to mention an excessive push for innovation demanding that any initiative, including branding campaigns, must be obviously different from those of the previous year. This line of thinking is a serious threat to the important need for brand consistency and reinforcement. The goal of all branding work is to win "mindshare", a term in the field of communications that is like market share, referring to the "share" that your brand can "occupy" in the minds of your target audiences – of course, the larger the share, the better. The trouble is that mindshare, like Rome, was not built in a day.

Perhaps the most significant point about the way forward for state-led branding initiatives is to take a leaf from the way that the "Garden City" brand positioning has sprouted so fruitfully over the decades. While the imagery of gardens has been employed, and indeed exploited, sometimes with

basically utilitarian motivations, the outcomes of the branding – its "proof points", in the jargon of the branding trade
– have developed organically. Pruning plants can be honed
towards a precise science, but whether the elements of Nature
can be coaxed to all conspire to produce the desired harvest
remains an art. In the same way, fostering the development
of "softer" facets of Singapore, from its human development
approach to its culture and arts, must similarly allow for a
degree of natural germination and flowering. In such areas,
the state – as it tries to move from a more directive function
as architect or engineer to a more facilitative role as farmer
or catalyst – can (and should) only do so much, and ought
to leave the rest to natural forces. Whether state actors can
resist the temptation to temper and to tamper is the question.
And whether, in Singapore's case, this has placed too many
limitations on what the private sector has achieved, and can
contribute, in nation branding, is something the next chapter
will seek to assess.

CHAPTER 3

BEYOND THE SINGAPORE GIRL

The brand promise and positioning
of Singapore Inc.

IN THE 1990s, the term "Singapore Inc." was used by Singapore's top politicians as a political metaphor for the whole country: the government played the role of "top management", as in a multinational company; the people (including resident foreigners) were its shareholders; and the country's trading partners its customers and business associates. Since around the start of the 21st century, this analogy has become used much less often.

In cases where it is still used – very rarely now – it refers not to the whole country but, more specifically, to that substantial portion of the economy owned and/or steered, directly or indirectly, by the government, such as through the investment holding company, Temasek Holdings.[1] More recently, "Singapore Inc." has been replaced with other political metaphors, such as "Team Singapore",[2] drawn from the world of sport, with the idea of the whole country striving as a contingent, like one sent to the Olympics, to compete in various sports and achieve excellence at different levels of competition.

There may be a few reasons for the decline in usage of the term "Singapore Inc.". One is that some metaphors simply go out of fashion. Another is that, in recent years, direct government participation in business has been deliberately de-emphasised, in response to negative reactions to the dominance of these entities in their respective industry sectors at home as well as, more obviously, overseas. Examples include the listed government-linked companies Keppel Corporation and CapitaLand, which have become dominant players mostly in Singapore's areas of traditional strength in "brick and mortar" infrastructure – logistics and building construction.

Perhaps more importantly, in nation branding terms, the focus has always been more foreign than local. Brand propositions have typically marketed Singapore much more as a "five-star location" or host for foreign companies, rather than as an attractive *exporter* through its independent home-grown enterprises. Singapore has even been likened to a top hotel, where investors can just come in and "plug and play". Companies that are not linked to the government or to Temasek Holdings have mostly been left to their own devices, although there have been calls over the years for more government support to help these companies "hunt in a pack"[3] for business opportunities overseas.

Reclaiming "Singapore Inc."?

In this chapter, the term "Singapore Inc." is used in the more literal and limited economic sense of referring to the republic's corporate sector as a whole. It is something of a missed opportunity that the term "Singapore Inc." has never quite been used in this way previously in public discourse. But this situation must change. For Singapore's corporate sector to fulfil its latent potential to add value to nation branding, this gap needs to be filled. Singaporean companies must be prouder to be Singaporean and to proclaim this branding much more loudly than they have done before. There ought to be a stronger sense of national unity, felt and displayed abroad and to international audiences. There is a need to reclaim the "natural meaning" of the concept of "Singapore Inc." in the economic sense.

To begin with, Singapore, despite its small size, does have corporate players who are branding giants in the world of global business who show that it can be done. As a Singapore Inc. bearer of nation branding to all the world, nobody beats Singapore Airlines. Its customer and branding reach cannot be challenged, carrying the flag and everything else in branding capacity that the carrier can convey to over 60 cities in some 35 countries. The important role played by SIA is emphasised by the fact that, for many people who have yet to visit Singapore, the airline is as close as they will ever get to seeing and feeling the essence of the Singapore brand; and on this score, Singapore has a tremendous track record. Much has been said about the brand attributes of Singapore Airlines[4] since the airline was set up in 1972, after Malaysia and Singapore went their separate ways with their national carriers following Singapore's independence in 1965. Since then, whether in innovation, cutting-edge technology or customer service, the airline has done extremely well to stay ahead of the pack in the branding game.

Singapore Airlines is one brand – one of a small number in the world – that has delivered on its brand promise consistently over the years, so much so that one of its recent advertising campaigns described the carrier as "the world's most awarded airline" – a badge of brand recognition to be proud of. The airline's many awards include *The Wall Street Journal Asia*'s "most admired Singapore company" accolade for many consecutive years. The key to success is never to rest on one's laurels, that is to say, to never forget the inherently brief lifespan of any brand advantage, and so, to invest relentlessly in research and development, innovation and improvement, so as to always keep two or three steps clear of the competition. This brand attribute itself is a key country brand characteristic of Singapore – summed up in the expression "only the paranoid survive", from remarks attributed to Andrew S. Grove, former chairman of Intel Corporation, and captured in the classic book of management and leadership, *Only The Paranoid Survive*.[5]

For Singapore Airlines, its brand essence has been distilled into a person: the Singapore Girl. In this "sensory branding" approach, the Singapore Girl brand has assumed a special "aura", a life of its own. The brand attributes include grace, elegance, warmth, consideration and sex appeal. The icon grew so strong that Madame Tussauds in London started displaying the Singapore Girl as a wax figure in 1994 as the first commercial figure ever – this is quite a coup, taking into account the considerations of nationalism, heritage and perceptions of commercialisation that must have weighed in on that decision. The occasion attracted wide international media attention.[6] The Singapore Girl remains as powerful an icon now as the day she was first introduced as the airline's ultimate brand ambassador.

Today, however, questions about the brand still revolve around the aspect of brand promise – the scope of sustaining the brand into the future. And here, it can be argued, with some justification, that the Singapore Girl's contribution to nation branding was stronger in the earlier years because it was more focused – in the sense that the majority of Singapore Girls were really Singapore girls, as in, citizens of the republic. Because of this, the brand positioning and messaging was also more authentic and clear. Today, with more women of other nationalities wearing the *kebaya* uniform – styled by the French *haute couture* designer Pierre Balmain – this increasing cosmopolitanisation of the Singapore Girl may, if not managed well, dilute the branding to some extent. Somehow, as a passenger on an SIA flight, whatever input you are getting in terms of your subconscious assessment of the Singapore country brand cannot but be affected if the stewardess who is serving you your Singapore Sling is not a Singaporean but from your own country – whether that is China, India or elsewhere – and speaks with the same accent.

With the phenomenon of more non-native Singapore Girls from non-traditional sources such as Thailand, the essential input to nation branding is channelled away from nationality and more to the more fundamental elements such as the whole image of the Singapore Girl (beyond the nationality of the stewardess) as well as the other aspects of service and standards that continue to set SIA apart, to make it – as one of its advertising taglines used to say – something "that even other airlines talk about". How to integrate foreign-born Singapore Girls might become a key branding challenge going forward, both for the airline and for the nation.

Indeed, the Singapore Girl remains so relevant that she has even been updated for modern times. In 2015, a new SIA stewardess became the second model for the Madame Tussaud's wax figure for the Singapore museum, opened on Sentosa in 2014. Perhaps more in keeping with what is perceived today as a more sensitive reflection of a broader range of expressions of femininity, the new model chosen is a Malay mother aged in her 30s with unusually short hair.[7] In the eyes of those who are more influenced by worldviews informed by ideas of challenging sexism, patriarchy and privilege, especially after the advent of the international #MeToo movement, the Singapore Girl might seem like a long overdue target.[8] But she actually is a counter-example to these perceptions, and reflects, arguably, the ironically higher place for women in Asia, supposedly a region of "less enlightened" societal norms. Far from being "demeaned" by the famous demands of looks, personal grooming and service quality, the Singapore Girl is looked up to as a model of grace and poise. If anything, to rebut the feminist argument, it is men, not the women, of SIA who are "demeaned" – because the stewards are the ones being accorded less attention and recognition than their female colleagues, who are much more appreciated and admired.

Associated with the branding success of the Singapore Girl is that of Changi Airport, which is part of the supporting infrastructure that enabled Singapore Airlines to become so profitable and thus able to invest in branding the way it did. Building on the string of industry accolades that Changi Airport has collected over the years and the strong Singapore branding, Changi Airports International, the group's subsidiary that manages overseas ventures and operations in countries including Russia and Saudi Arabia, and provides consultancy to countries ranging from China to as far as Uganda.

The Singapore name, riding on the reliability and success of operations in Singapore, has also supported an international network of operations in other sectors. In port management and the shipping business, for example, PSA International manages ports from Argentina to Panama; and Ascendas looks after industrial land and business space from Vietnam to Oman. There are yet other areas of specialised exportable expertise, including the management of reclaimed industrial land in a facility like Jurong Island, fashioned out of seven offshore islands to create a home for leading companies in petroleum, petrochemicals, specialty chemicals and manufacturing. Another example is public housing, with Singapore's Housing and Development Board (HDB) developing more expertise that other countries seek to learn from, even as it has won accolades such as the United Nations-Habitat Scroll of Honour Award for providing one of the world's greenest, cleanest and most socially conscious public housing programmes.

In many markets, the Singapore name alone gets you through the front door. Singapore's corporate players have benefited from the positive mindshare created from decades of successful nation branding. "Made in Singapore" carries a certain cachet, as Singaporean companies are seen to have some good qualities hard-wired into their "corporate DNA" – to be honest, trustworthy and reliable – just as Swiss and German companies are believed to be efficient and quality-conscious by nature. Quite aside from the republic's inherent locational advantages, which are plain to see, Singapore's many decades of facilitating multinational companies and other investors to do business in Singapore have enabled it to build up expertise that has won many accolades, as well as a huge pool of clientele who reinforce the state's own nation branding efforts with even more valuable customer endorsement and recommendation by word of mouth. These advantages, based on an impressive track record, can only grow stronger.

In the wake of Covid-19's devastation of vast swathes of the world economy, sights are being set on the growth areas that will emerge in the early periods of tentative recovery. One of the policy tools in government hands will be to see how and where to boost economic activity with infrastructure projects. One shift from before would be in domestic areas of previous shortfall or neglect, instead of ambitious building ahead of demand as before. China is one place where building and construction could see more focus, and here, there may be opportunities for corporate entities from Singapore in the years to come.

Raffles: Selling a brand

If the Singapore Girl is quintessentially Singaporean, the same cannot exactly be said of another icon – the Raffles Hotel. "It is the end of an era," reported the *Financial Times*, when the Raffles Hotel was sold in 2005.[9] After 118 years, the colonial institution entered the portfolio of the US investment firm Colony Capital, rubbing shoulders with US casinos and London's Savoy Group. The vendor, CapitaLand, owner of Raffles Holdings, booked a US$360-million gain from exiting its hotel business. The question is whether things have changed since in terms of brand essence.

Of course, to many observers, the essentials are still there: The ambience of a stately hotel that symbolised "all the fables of the exotic east" to the 19th-century novelist W. Somerset Maugham. The turbaned doorman who opens the door of your limousine as you step onto the gravel driveway on Beach Road. All these, and more, are still there. Raffles Hotel is a national landmark. Just as no visitor to Paris would leave without at least catching sight of the Eiffel Tower, so too, every tourist to Singapore would have on their must-do list visiting the hotel and enjoying a Singapore Sling – a gin-based cocktail developed sometime before 1915 by bartender Ngiam Tong Boon – at the Long Bar.

Beneath it all, however, something may have slipped away, at least for now. In its latest refurbishment, opened in 2019, the restaurants have been changed by the French company that now manages the hotel. Some old favourite spots, like the Writers' Bar and Tiffin Room, remain. But the Bar and Billiard Room is no more. More importantly, for Singapore's nation branding, the big loss was in branding control by

Singaporeans of the Singapore landmark itself, as well as the international branding afforded by all the properties of the Raffles Holdings group, which once stretched from Praslin, Seychelles, to Makkah, Saudi Arabia. To no longer have the Singapore flag fluttering 24/7 from flagpoles in the hotels' driveways is to lose major platforms of nation branding that cannot be measured in dollars and cents. Ironically though, the terms of dollars and cents was how the gain-and-loss equation was calculated in that landmark sale in 2005. The sale of Raffles Hotel is typical of Singapore – pragmatic and hard-nosed to a fault, which is itself a key aspect of its nation branding. The underlying logic applied by the sellers was that there is more value in the money realised through selling Raffles than there was in retaining control over the brand direction. It has been said that the key consideration here was return on equity, and not "return on emotion", dismissing concerns over the loss of a key Singaporean brand as an emotional reaction. But the point is also that a country's iconic brands belong not just to shareholders but also to the stakeholders, the citizens. For sure, the extent of abstract value in having control over an iconic brand remains debatable, but certainly, something was lost even as something was gained.

The brand Raffles may no longer be in Singaporean hands, but all is not lost, some might argue. The returns from selling Raffles were invested partly into real estate in China – and that investment is now reaping a different outcome in nation branding for Singapore. Today, CapitaLand's logo is gaining more recognition by the day as it dots the skyline, emblazoned on buildings such as Raffles City in Shanghai and other cities in the world's fastest-growing economy. As the *Financial Times* put it: "Less romantic than Raffles, perhaps, but commercially more attractive". The most recent Raffles City Chongqing mall, CapitaLand's ninth Raffles City development in China that opened in 2019, has a similar design to the Marina Bay Sands Singapore. This is not surprising since the designer is the same: Moshe Safdie, the architect behind Marina Bay Sands and Changi Airport's Jewel.

More recently, the hard image of unsentimental pragmatism that such projects portray has been softened to some extent by CapitaLand's greater involvement in corporate social responsibility initiatives through its philanthropic arm, CapitaLand Hope Foundation. The foundation was set up in 2005 to build schools, hospitals and homes for the less-privileged young in China, and to sponsor the development of educational opportunities and other facilities. This has been joined by other efforts such as that of CapitaLand's parent, Temasek Holdings, which, through its Temasek Foundation, is reaching out even further into the region on behalf of Singapore, with initiatives in China that also touch other sectors including journalism and academia with its support for activities such as visit programmes, conferences and research collaboration projects.

Nation branding through foreign aid and philanthropy is an example of how much a country can gain by becoming more active in its fulfilment of its corporate social responsibility, or just "social responsibility" in this case, as a nation. It is a parallel to how doing more CSR is good for a corporate organisation. This new track of nation branding has been seen as more viable and fruitful ever since Singapore, as a "parent company" through its sovereign wealth fund, began to find it trickier, and more treacherous, to act as any more overt and ostentatious a brand steward and standard-bearer for Singapore, along with its business expansion efforts into other countries.

Projecting this potential further, Singapore has a typical instinct to excel and win in everything it sets out to do, and the deep desire to be Number One in all things. These, in themselves, are quintessential brand attributes that are so distinctive that a uniquely Singaporean term has been coined for it, *kiasuism* (fear of losing out). Now, imagine what Singapore could achieve if it put its manpower and money into the pursuit of its "national CSR". Here, an organisation like the Singapore International Foundation – a non-profit body set up in 1991 to connect Singapore to the world for sustainable development, international understanding and uplifting lives[10] – could do much more to enhance Singapore's nation branding. It has done, and is doing, good work in areas such as promoting international volunteerism for Singaporeans, but needs to get the word out even more prominently and effectively. If Singapore were to truly place "national CSR" high on its national priorities, this would be quite some brand makeover for this "GDP city", from its traditional obsession with material, quantifiable objectives that can quickly boost the GDP. If it ever became as single-minded in investing in national CSR as in other aspects of nation-building, Singapore would be any CSR advocate's dream nation. There were missed opportunities in this area during the Covid-19 crisis, which will be discussed further in Chapter 7 on the future.

Time for a Tiger

Partly as a consequence of Singapore's reliance on manufacturing as the key engine of growth for the first 45 years of its modern economic history, there are relatively few consumer brands that have become well-known internationally. There were two major driving forces for this. First, the primary emphasis in the 20th century was always in supporting the growth of industry in manufacturing activity such as electronics, engineering and chemicals, and manufacturing-related services such as logistics, leading to less support for other sectors. Second, in the 20th century, tourism and tourism-related industries such as retail and food and beverage were relatively less emphasised in all aspects, including policy, funding and certainly branding.

Non-government-linked consumer companies were left to build their brands on their own. Thus, aside from Singapore Airlines, Tiger Beer is one of the few other major brands that people would mention in the same breath as having anything approaching the same worldwide reach as SIA. Like Raffles Hotel, the Tiger brand has also ceded control to foreign hands, with the Dutch brewer Heineken buying up the stake owned by Asia Pacific Breweries, the parent company of Tiger that had previously been run jointly by Heineken and Fraser & Neave since 1931. Needless to say, Tiger Beer is not in the same league as Singapore Airlines, in the sense that far fewer people who have heard of the beer know that it is Singaporean, or have top-of-mind recall of this detail. There *are* branding efforts and platforms overseas, such as the Tiger Beer Singapore Chilli Crab Festival, which has been held on the Brooklyn waterfront in New York, as well as in London and Dubai. But such cases of prominent and direct identification of Tiger Beer with Singapore are comparatively few and far between, when placed alongside the very clear and widespread brand association of Singapore Airlines with its home country. Nonetheless, the market and audience reach already achieved by Tiger Beer means that each time a member of its existing brand audience makes the connection with Singapore, Singapore gains much immediate "retroactive benefit" in positive nation branding.

This is the ultimate benefit to nation branding from Tiger Beer's international standing. Since its birth in 1932, the brand has become one of the most distinctive Asian icons in the global arena. Today, Tiger Beer is brewed in 11 countries from Cambodia to Papua New Guinea, and is available in the US and over 70 other countries across Europe,

Latin America, Australia and the Middle East. The beer has also won awards such as the Brewing Industry International Award in Britain in 1998, the gold medal in the European Style Pilsener category of the 2004 World Beer Cup and a gold medal at the New Zealand International Beer Awards in 2008. In the US, Tiger Beer has won rave reviews as the leading premium brew from Asia. Tiger is now available in 48 of the country's 50 states. The beer has also gained considerable popularity in Detroit because of the Detroit Tigers, a Major League baseball team that shares Tiger Beer's name and colours. In Britain, Tiger topped a list of 50 top beer brands in 2004, and is served at more than 8,000 bars, clubs and distribution outlets in major cities such as London, Manchester, Leeds and Newcastle. England footballer Wayne Rooney was the star of a Tiger Beer TV advertisement that aired in Asia during the 2010 soccer World Cup in South Africa. Other celebrities who have endorsed Tiger Beer include American actress Jessica Alba, who starred in a TV ad in 2005 – something the company claims makes Tiger Beer "the first Singapore brand to be endorsed by a Hollywood celebrity".[11] Tiger Beer even has the benefit of a long heritage and popularity in the Malay peninsula that it can claim stretching back into colonial times. The English author Anthony Burgess adored Tiger Beer so much that he named one of his novels after the beer's advertising slogan of the time: "Time for a Tiger". *Time for a Tiger* is Part One of Burgess' Malayan Trilogy, *The Long Day Wanes*, set in the twilight of British rule over the peninsula. It was Burgess' first published work of fiction and appeared in 1956.

Having conquered the formidable Western markets with a branding mix of brand attributes wrapped around a brew of exoticism and excellence, Tiger Beer is on the prowl for more, this time in a fast-expanding Asia, especially in the burgeoning consumer market in China. Singaporean food brands that are currently in China include Bee Cheng Hiang, Brand's, Eu Yan Sang, Gold Kili, Prima Food, Super Coffee-mix and Yeo Hiap Seng in addition to Tiger Beer. There is still some brand value from the recognition of Tiger as a Singa-porean brand, but, as with Raffles, without control over the brand direction, things will certainly never be the same again. The difference can be described like this: For the best place branding, it is not enough just to have domain knowledge, which outsiders can always acquire. What matters more is the heart and sensibility of a practitioner who truly knows – and yes, loves – the place.

Celebrity rub-off effect

Aside from Tiger Beer, few other homegrown Singaporean companies have grabbed international attention. Thus, for now at least, it may still be left to foreign international brands to add to Singapore's nation branding. If Singapore is known for anything above all, it is as a place for doing business. Excel-lent infrastructure, a pro-business government, harmonious labour relations, political stability, flexible policies geared for business, a responsive manpower pool – these are just some of the pluses that other countries find difficult to match, much less replicate. In this environment, the MNCs based in Singapore effectively become avenues for the republic to brand itself to the thousands of people who work for, and do business with, these firms.

One of the biggest of these branding platforms ever for Singapore was when the oil giant Caltex relocated its global headquarters to the Lion City from Irving, Texas, in 1998. However, Singapore lost that global HQ status in the wake of the October 2001 merger of the two oil majors Chevron and Texaco – Caltex's two parent companies – into Chevron-Texaco, following which the group's global headquarters was moved back to San Ramon, California. Although Singapore remains one of the company's three global hubs, together with London and Houston, this was certainly a lost opportunity to build on the global branding platform that Caltex's global HQ would have provided, to draw even more companies to base their HQ operations in the republic.[12] In 2011, the semiconductor parts maker Kulicke & Soffa moved its global HQ from Philadelphia, USA, to Singapore,[13] and this move, while not on the scale of a Caltex, might encourage other companies to also make Singapore their global home.

More recently, Singapore's attractiveness as a corporate location shone again when British technology company Dyson (most famous to the layman for its high-tech vacuum cleaners) made international headlines in announcing in 2019 that it would be moving its global headquarters to Singapore.[14] In quintessential British style, the location selected is the heritage building of St James Power Station. Constructed in 1927, the building housed Singapore's first coal-fired power plant, built by the British, before falling into disuse and then being turned into an entertainment complex and nightlife hub. In 2009, it was declared a national monument.

Since 1961 – when the Economic Development Board was established – Singapore has thrived on attracting outstanding foreign companies to set up operations in the republic.[15] In decades past, the spotlight was on electronics companies, such as Hewlett-Packard, and oil companies, such as Shell. More recently, the focus has shifted from industries in the hard sciences to "softer" disciplines such as digital animation. Industries do not come softer than the make-believe world of fantasy in Lucasfilm Ltd, founded by filmmaker George Lucas of *Star Wars* fame, which opened a 60,000-square-foot Singapore studio in 2005. The Singapore office now employs staff from over 40 countries and has done computer graphics work for films such as *Iron Man 2* and the animated TV series *Star Wars: The Clone Wars*. The Asian location allowed the company to create a 24-hour production cycle, so that work being done in California could carry on in Singapore overnight. For many reasons, Singapore was an obvious choice[16]: The country is English-speaking, tech-savvy, and ideally located to tap the talent pool and technology tie-ups from around Southeast Asia and India. Government grants and attentive assistance were also a great help, for sure.

In the short term, it will be foreign companies like Lucasfilm that will have the immediate capacity to add significantly to Singapore's nation branding with what is the equivalent of a "corporate celebrity rub-off" effect.

Peranakan culture and the appetite for more

The big picture that emerges on the corporate front is one of untapped potential, of how much more "Singapore Inc." could become. Singapore is gaining more recognition as the food capital of Asia, where some of the best Asian and international chefs and restaurants can be found. But while this attracts a sizeable chunk of visitors to Singapore, there is a gap between Singaporeans' love for food and dining, and the vacuum that exists in terms of Singaporean chefs, restaurant owners and other food and beverage-related businesses that have made it big globally, or even now have the capacity to aim to do so, especially in the wake of Covid-19. In other words, the attraction is mostly all inward, but outward expansion is not that much to speak of. Passion is certainly made possible at home in Singapore, but outside these shores, it is usually a different story. For example, Tee Yih Jia, headquartered in Singapore, stakes a claim as the world's largest producer of *popiah* (spring roll) skins, and this certainly can make a mark in its industry sector, but even then, just as with other homegrown brands, its products are not always known as Singaporean.

The existing gulf in achievement by Singaporeans in the food and beverage industry is huge, compared with the universal popularity and presence of, say, Chinese, Japanese or Thai food. Even Malaysia is represented by the Penang chain of restaurants that has opened in many major US cities. There are Singapore restaurants in places such as London and Boston, but these are, in terms of relative size and branding mindshare among international audiences, at best as tiny as a titbit of finger food in relation to the global market share of world cuisine. Most of them are small, family-run businesses, with no real immediate scope for scaling up. And this is not entirely due to any shortage of ambition or ability. To really make it big would require the support of a big-enough clientele, existing and potential. And the size of this clientele, in turn, depends on there being enough brand awareness and brand acceptance of the entire culture represented by that cuisine internationally.

Currently, that larger backdrop is still missing for Singapore, not least because there is no one major culture it can claim as its own. The most unique is Peranakan culture, which has some potential to be explored for its distinctive qualities. For example, a full experience of "cultural immersion" could be offered in a manner that Japanese *ryokans* have made famous – Singapore inns decorated completely in Peranakan style, at which guests, upon checking in, can slip on batik robes and enjoy authentic Peranakan food and drink after their traditional bath.[17] Peranakan cuisine is enjoying something of a renaissance in Singapore in the 2010s, with more restaurants than ever before in the country's history, from small restaurants offering home-cooked fare to Michelin-starred fine cuisine. The ambition and new-found cultural confidence are evidenced, for example, in the audacious naming of the restaurant National Kitchen.

However, the fact that Peranakan food is not truly unique – its origins are mostly shared with Malaysia – is less important than that it is perhaps too "niche" to have a critical mass of customer support. Hypothetically, an opportunity may lie in Singaporean restaurants offering a substantial menu of Chinese, Indian, Malay, Peranakan, Eurasian and Western cuisine all at once – something that most restaurants would not do, as specialisation is the preferred business model. Offering such a variety all in one place – and doing it really well, the way Singapore Airlines builds its brand – could be one way towards brand differentiation. It would also, from a sociological perspective, exemplify a key brand attribute of Singapore itself – its cosmopolitanism and unique brand of multiculturalism, blended and preserved and presented well, just like its cuisine.

The essential gaps discussed so far in this chapter – what is missing in the larger backdrop for business in terms of such foundation elements as original content, confidence and support – perhaps sum up how much more can be achieved on the world stage by corporate players, if enough Singaporeans had the aspiration, assets and artistry to truly work to make a difference. Companies such as luxury resort developer Banyan Tree are doing very well as businesses internationally, but they could perhaps do more to specifically highlight their Singaporeanness. This could take the form of simple things like including Singaporean dishes on its resort restaurant menus, or highlighting in the welcome folder Singaporean heritage elements in the rooms' interior decor.

Some of what needs to be enhanced in the larger backdrop are beyond the control of the entrepreneurs themselves – such as the inherent disadvantages of lack of critical mass for Singaporean culture itself on the world stage. Still, the best role model of corporate nation branding globally for Singapore is there, as she has been all these years, for all to examine and emulate – the Singapore Girl, and all that she stands for and all that she has to back her. The ubiquity of this very individual symbol of nation branding places some responsibility on the svelte shoulders of every Singaporean woman who wears the signature Balmain *sarong kebaya* to play her part in nation branding. It is a strong yet vulnerable image to bear in mind, as the focus turns in the next chapter to the part played by ordinary Singaporeans in making up, and adding to, brand Singapore.

CHAPTER 4

THE PEOPLE'S ACTION PARTLY – UNTIL "SG50"

Cultural capital and Singaporeans'
contributions to nation branding

T THE CANNES Film Festival in April 2010, a Singapore-made movie, *Sandcastle*, directed by Boo Junfeng, was one of seven films at the festival's International Critics' Week. It marked the sixth consecutive year that a Singapore film had been featured at Cannes, the global industry's leading festival. In his review, the British film critic Tony Rayns commented that the movie "hits the heart as hard as it challenges the state".[1] As any branding exponent would tell you, anything that can hit the heart that hard should be pretty powerful branding. Three years later, Singapore went further, with the movie *Ilo Ilo* directed by Anthony Chen winning the Camera d'Or prize for best first feature film at the 2013 Cannes Film Festival. The 2017 Singaporean-Thai movie *Pop Aye,* directed by Kirsten Tan, won four awards at the Sundance Film Festival and was Singapore's submission to the 2018 Academy Awards in the Foreign Language Film category.[2] At a deeper level, the film – set in Thailand and with the dialogue almost entirely in Thai – also marks a new level of confidence in Singapore's filmmakers in venturing beyond the island for their material. It is fair to say that Singapore cinema has arrived on the world stage.

Such significant examples of Singaporean cultural products have made their contributions in their own ways to the country's nation branding. Like the employees of a corporation, the people from a country are, ultimately, its most important brand ambassadors. For example, consider the way that Americans are among the most fervent ambassadors for their country brand, both internally and externally. In most countries, visitors looking for an official building look out for the national flag – which would serve you well in Singapore. But doing this in the USA would not be much help, because practically every commercial building, and many residential premises too, display the flag proudly and prominently all year round. As external brand ambassadors, Americans' gestures range from an overall pervasive instinct to advocate American core values such as freedom and democracy wherever they get an opportunity – sometimes too loudly – to small actions like wearing American flag lapel pins on their jackets everywhere they go.

In Singapore, however, the people generally tend to play a uniquely circumscribed role, although this is slowly changing. In this chapter, the spotlight is turned on the input to Singapore's nation branding from people and organisations that are not part of the government or business sector. The title of this chapter is a play on the name of the only ruling political party that independent Singapore has ever known – the People's Action Party. The word "partly" describes the much less powerful role performed by citizen actors in the great play that is nation branding over the years, compared with the (sometimes overwhelming) dominance of initiatives led by government, and government-linked, agencies. In the past, the people of Singapore had been perceived as having a creativity deficit, relative to other societies better-known for artistry and inventiveness, from the USA to, nearer home, South Korea. The basis for this could be attributed mainly to a cultural norm of valuing social order as a foundation for everything else. An outcome of this is an ingrained social discipline, which will be a societal asset in the process of tackling, and eventually emerging from, the Covid-19 pandemic. This brand attribute of discipline is further honed, for men, through compulsory national service. The subjugation of self to the larger cause of duty to the nation is captured in these lines from my poem *The Fragrance of Lallang* in *From Boys to Men,* a literary anthology of national service:[3]

> *"the more we sweat in peace,*
> *the less we bleed in war":*
> *so the motivational slogans sell*
> *a logic you can almost smell*

Coupled with other pervasive socio-political constraints on freedom of expression, it is fair to say that Singaporeans did not contribute as much as they could to the nation brand in the earlier decades. But all this changed in 2015.

"SG50": The game-changer

The rather more limited participation of the common man in building the country brand all changed with "SG50" in 2015, the year of celebrations for Singapore's golden jubilee of independence as a sovereign nation. The motivations for the year-long array of events and activities were decidedly political and social. Nation brand-building was a secondary aspect, if it was overtly considered at all. But in the process, the people of Singapore were actually being engaged in thinking about the country brand, and in adding to the nation brand on an unprecedented scale.

An "SG50" logo was created – with "SG" on top of "50" in red lettering, inside a white circle with a red border, playing with the idea of Singapore as "a little red dot". This phrase was derived from an expression attributed in 1998 to former Indonesian president B.J. Habibie, about Singapore being just "a little red dot" on the world map. Since then, this "nickname" has been embraced by Singaporeans themselves as a term of endearment, a reminder of how Singapore has transcended its limited physical size to reach for global achievements in many areas. Beyond the celebratory year of 2015, a variation of this logo continues to be in use, now just as "SG" without the "50", to celebrate the many facets of the "Singapore spirit". This "SG" logo will also be a new "central focus" of Singapore's downtown of the future as the flooring design of the NS Square platform, a new community space set to be redeveloped from the existing The Float @ Marina Bay by 2025.

With "SG50", an interest in heritage was boosted universally, with some 400 projects initiated by citizens capturing memories and promoting nostalgia, from time capsules to "looking back" publications. Pioneers in all spheres of life and all kinds of "icons" of Singapore were profiled, from local foods like *rojak* to childhood images of dragon-shaped playgrounds in Toa Payoh housing estate. In all these ways, the whole "SG50" year was truly a game-changer in rousing and engaging the energies of ordinary Singaporeans in the way they thought about brand Singapore, if only indirectly and subconsciously. As Finance Minister Heng Swee Keat, who headed the "SG50" steering committee, said, the SG50 year sparked a new Singapore spirit and gave the people a greater sense of home: "That to me is the biggest achievement of "SG50".[4] It is fair to say that the effect of "SG50" in creating and spreading awareness about national identity and Singapore's brand proposition was so pervasive and powerful that nothing will be the same again when it comes to citizen participation in shaping Singapore's country brand. A stirring of this strand of "active citizenry" to a much lesser extent was in force throughout the Bicentennial year of 2019 that was to follow four years later, to mark 200 years of the legacy of British colonialism. The cumulative effect of these two years of people engagement in dispelling the pervasive citizen docility of the previous five decades might even have been an underlying factor in the result of the 2020 general election, which is seen to reflect a clear desire for greater participation by the electorate in the country's political affairs.

Cultural capital and soft power

"Cultural capital" is a term in sociology usually used to refer to the intellectual and educational resources – knowledge, skills, qualifications – that can promote social mobility in a society, in the broad sense of thinkers such as the French sociologist Pierre Bourdieu, as a way to explain how power in society is transferred and social classes maintained.[5] Applied to nation branding, the term "cultural capital" can be used to refer to the stock of a nation's cultural products that help articulate and express its culture. This is "capital" in the sense that, when invested well, just like financial capital, there are rich payoffs for the rest of society. The key verbs here are "articulate" and "express" – as opposed to "define", as it may not be possible ever to "define" something as diffuse and amorphous as a culture.

"Soft power", a concept coined by Harvard Kennedy School professor Joseph Nye, refers to the ability of a country to influence other nations and international agendas by attracting admiration and agreement from others, and co-opting support and assistance in advancing a cause.[6] In contrast to "hard power", which is to have influence over others through the assertion of economic heft or military might, soft power can be expressed by government actors through diplomacy, strategic communications, foreign assistance, civic action and economic reconstruction and development. Expressed through citizen actors, soft power usually takes the form of some element of "cultural capital". The more distinctive and meaningful a country's cultural products, the more they influence the perceptions of audiences abroad. Cultural platforms like Hollywood and Netflix fulfil that role for the USA, and the stock of this cultural capital that can feed into the nation branding of America is rich indeed.

In a sense, the cultural divide could perhaps never be bridged because those cultures with a headstart are well-placed to build exponentially on their advantage, so that the gulf is widening all the time. For example, in the current ongoing geopolitical rivalry between the US and China, the American economy was more than twice that of China's at the start of the 21st century, notes Joseph Nye in his 2005 book *Soft Power: The Means to Success in World Politics*. But in soft power terms, the gap could be even greater, he adds, citing a line from my op-ed in Singapore's *Today* newspaper in 2004: "When it comes to soft power, it will take much longer before [China] can make an impact close to what the US enjoys now".[7] The famous always become even more famous.

In terms of a presence on such platforms, Singapore has an even longer way to go in terms of reducing – never mind closing – the gap with larger, older countries. But still, Singapore can certainly do more to boost its cultural portfolio. The total audience for Singapore-made cultural products may be small in a world full of people whose short attention spans are already filled with mostly imported American cultural products and a few others from their own cultures. In the 2010s, it appears that this balance is beginning to change in many countries, in that homegrown cultural products are gaining more mindshare, as the power of American soft power wanes around the world, with the decline of American prestige internationally. At the same time, audiences are becoming even more fragmented into mostly self-reinforcing communities or "bubbles" in the online universe. In such an environment, penetration by a foreign cultural soft power will depend on some "inside help".

Hence, if Singaporean cultural products could manage to influence even just a few opinion leaders in other countries, they would help Singapore become better-understood on several fronts – offering a deeper insight into Singapore society, challenging prejudice and stereotype, inviting closer observation of the true nature of the country, and contributing to the projection of Singapore's soft power into the international arena.

In today's more divided world, post-Brexit and under a Trump presidency in the USA with its "America first" stance, there are very clear signs that soft power is on the retreat and a shift back towards the pre-eminence of hard power has been underway for some time, with measures such as the introduction of trade tariffs, the jettisoning and realignment of trade deals by a USA pulling back from globalisation, along with many other countries in the wake of the spread of Covid-19, as well as with geopolitical shifts such as the assertion of military might in the South China Sea. At one level, soft power will find it harder to prevail against the weight of hard power. In the heat of a full-blown global trade war, concrete concerns that affect earnings and livelihoods will always trump other considerations.

Yet, on another level, those countries that continue to believe in the deeper, longer-lasting impact of soft power, and are able to apply it well, could get more opportunities to win more friends in a less friendly international environment. This would include countries like Canada that excel at promoting diversity, those like Japan that stand out in keeping political populism at bay, or those like Singapore that do a great job of preserving multicultural harmony. Hard power thrives best in market situations of monopoly. But given the increasing dispersion of bargaining power in a more fragmented world, nations that have something extra to offer – based on the nation brand equity they have earned with effective application of soft power – would also be better-placed to do well in a post-Covid-19 world.

Singlish: Last time not OK, now maybe can?

Anything that makes Singaporean cultural resources unique carries with it added potential to contribute to the country brand. Something distinctive also has the bonus of novelty. On this score, Singlish, the colloquial form of English used in informal contexts in Singapore, certainly has its place in the creation of uniquely Singaporean cultural material. It is a patois that generates much wit and creativity, an especially valuable element to connect with audiences of all forms of the arts and much of social media. This unique blend of Singaporean slang and English has its own grammar adapted from Singapore's other languages such as Chinese, as well as colourful vocabulary borrowed from the linguistic resources of other communities, especially Malay and Hokkien. Its characteristics are explained in books such as *Spiaking Sin-glish* by Gwee Li Sui.[8] Singlish adds value to brand Singapore by enlivening, and giving character to, much of the dialogue in Singapore-made movies, TV shows, stage plays, literature and, of course, standup comedy. It is a vital ingredient to foster identity and belonging.

Historically, Singlish has suffered from having an uncertain status in Singapore. In earlier decades, this often-misunderstood creole was officially discouraged, for fear that it would interfere with the learning of "proper" English, and so, hamper communication with the rest of the world, which would then, of course, affect the earning of GDP. Indeed, the authorities in charge of media regulation went so far as to set a time-cap on how many minutes of a film's dialogue could have Singlish in proportion to the film's whole duration, and civil servants would even go about calculating if this limit was breached. On the other hand, supporters of Singlish have always argued against such fears, pointing to the ability of Singlish users to code-switch to standard English in appropriate situations.

Every now and then, this debate resurfaces not only about Singlish but also anything "local" that foreigners might not understand. The divide appears to hinge on two contrasting worldviews about the arts. For example, in a *Straits Times* op-ed column in 1995, I disagreed with a reader's letter suggesting that the title of the 1995 Singapore movie *Mee Pok Man*, directed by Eric Khoo, should be translated into proper English to reach larger audiences overseas. My main argument was this: "Artists should not change aspects of their own culture to suit their audiences. It is up to audiences to make the effort to understand things foreign."[9] This is almost a cardinal rule of place branding – always be authentic; don't sacrifice authenticity to try to be more appealing to others, because what is also being sacrificed is identity.

Now, with Covid-19, one curious effect of the greater isolation of societies, brought about by the shutting down of national borders, could be to paradoxically give freer rein to the use of Singlish. To begin with, a world reeling from the worst pandemic of the century has adjusted to a new normal in which everyone agrees that getting the world back on its feet is more important than many things that people used to focus energy on, including trying to discourage the use of Singlish. Singapore's government agencies, seeking to send public health messages to a general public in partial pandemic lockdown, have themselves stepped up their use of Singlish. To reach the older, less well-educated generations, government communications have also used more Chinese dialects like Cantonese, which had been practically banned from public usage in earlier decades as part of the national effort to promote proficiency in Mandarin, also for economic benefits.

More importantly, at a time of closed borders, when the world outside seems further away, and there are also more pressing concerns than policing language use, there might actually be less effort to try to curb Singlish. Everyone has no option but to become more inward-looking, and so, more appreciative of what is homegrown, and also, more forgiving of earlier perceived flaws. Within such perceived "bubbles", people tend to behave more freely, as if talking amongst themselves. At the same time, others feel that those who use Singlish are able to "do less harm" than before, from being cut off from the rest of the world. Hence, they would do less to try to deter such "improper behaviour". Thus, the constraints of Covid-19 might actually free up Singlish more, and so, prompt brand Singapore, along with all other place brands, towards a deeper, richer authenticity.

On screen and stage

Of all the forms of cultural capital, film has probably been the most powerful. Singapore films have been screened, and have won recognition, at film festivals such as Busan in Korea, New York, Toronto – and Cannes, still the main esteem arena for the global film industry. Singapore's representation at Cannes began with Eric Khoo's movie about life in Singapore's urban heartlands, *12 Storeys*, in 1997, when it was chosen to be showcased in the Un Certain Regard section. Khoo returned in 2005 with the film *Be With Me*, which opened the Director's Fortnight. The floodgates were officially opened the following year when 12 Singapore films were presented at the World Cinema programme. Then came Pok Yue Weng's short film *SuperDong* in the Director's Fortnight, Ekachai Uekrongtham's feature *Pleasure Factory* in the Un Certain Regard section, and the Special Mention award-winning short film *Ah Ma* by Anthony Chen in 2007. In 2008, Khoo scored a hat-trick when *My Magic* became the first Singapore film to compete for the coveted Palme d'Or award, and in 2009, filmmaker and visual artist Ho Tzu Nyen's experimental film, *Here*, was shown at the Director's Fortnight.[10]

The Singapore film at Cannes in 2010, *Sandcastle*, will continue to attract international attention for an important added reason: The movie's theme of Chinese-school student protests in the 1950s surfaces Chinese cultural issues that are still relevant in Singapore today, and connects it with one of the most prominent themes in global current affairs – the rise of China. In the past, most people considered that Singapore films "could not travel" because they dealt with themes such as life in an HDB housing estate in a way that international audiences could not identify with easily. Filmmaker Boo Junfeng has continued to make an impact, winning the Rising Director Award for his critically acclaimed film, *Apprentice*, at the 2016 Busan International Film Festival's Asia Star Awards.

In future, the Singaporean movie-makers who connect with the largest international audiences possible will be those who can address universal and global concerns, tackling themes such as that of *Mad About English* (2008), directed by Lian Pek, about the craze to learn English in China, the biggest consumer and cultural market today. To take another example, the movie *Singapore Dreaming* (2006), directed by Woo Yen Yen and Colin Goh, might have done better if it had invited more overt comparison of its theme with the universally known American Dream. By that same token, while Jack Neo is probably, going by sheer numbers, the most influential movie-maker to domestic audiences and the Mandarin-speaking world for his more superficial slapstick comedies, it is only with enough deeper critical assessment that his better films such as *I Not Stupid* (2002) – a critique of the education system and social stratification – could really add to nation branding.

Singaporean theatre has also contributed to nation branding, with local practitioners taking their work overseas, and in the process shaping outsiders' perceptions of Singapore. Ong Keng Sen, for example, has presented his plays and curated festivals in cities including Tokyo, Berlin and London. The 2003 Cultural Medallion winner has a Distinguished Artist Award from the New York-based International Society for the Performing Arts, and in 2007 was appointed a Regents' Lecturer by the University of California, Los Angeles, a prestigious post given to distinguished individuals from non-academic fields. Indeed, Ong is "so often perceived as the face of Singapore theatre that some overseas festival organisers feel they have 'done Singapore' as long as they have invited him before".[11] In 1988, Ong became artistic director of the theatre company Theatreworks, set up in 1985. But it was not until 1997 that one could truly say a platform for nation branding was created, when he benefited from the sponsorship of the Asia Centre of the Japan Foundation, to create *Lear*, an intercultural performance of the Shakespearean tragedy using traditional and contemporary arts performers that went on to tour eight cities in Asia, Europe and Australia. The production became the first part of his Asian Shakespeare Trilogy, which also includes *Desdemona* (2000) and *Search: Hamlet* (2002). Ong continued to present faces of Singapore through theatre in his role as Director of the Singapore International Festival of Arts for four years from 2013.

Like Ong, Glen Goei has put Singapore on the map in world theatre, and now, also in film. He is still the only Singaporean to have made a prominent mark on the theatre scene in London's West End, starring in the title role alongside Anthony Hopkins in the Tony Award-winning play *M. Butterfly* in 1989. He went on to be the artistic director of Mu-Lan Arts in London from 1990 to 1998. It was the first Asian theatre company to be established in Britain and won awards for fringe theatre. More recently, he has made waves internationally in film, perhaps drawn to this medium by its larger audiences. Goei's 1998 film *Forever Fever* was the first Singapore film to achieve a worldwide commercial release, distributed in the US and Britain by Miramax. His 2009 movie *The Blue Mansion* was screened at film festivals in Busan, Tokyo and Hong Kong, and shown at other events such as the Singapour Festivarts programme in Paris in 2010.

Commenting on the Singapore festival in Paris, Christophe Girard, deputy mayor of Paris, said that Singapore is often perceived as a "monied and culturally arid" city like Monaco and Luxembourg, but in fact, "it is a city of millions of people who have culture, history and work, who are from various origins" and who have "a voice" expressed through culture and the arts.[12] As Goei's career progression from stage to screen is suggesting, film may yet turn out to be the more powerful medium for global nation branding for Singapore.

Singapore stories

In the field of the written word, the best-known contributor to nation branding to international audiences would have to be the novelist Catherine Lim. In the late 1990s, by adding on the role of political commentator and one of the few vocal critics of the ruling party, she further enhanced her prominence.[13] Lim's more than 20 books of prose and poetry have been published in a dozen countries, including the novel *Following The Wrong God Home* published by British publisher Orion. The added point of international interest – and it is quite a significant one, given the Western media's typical focus on the topic of political dissent – emerged after what has been dubbed "the Catherine Lim affair" in 1994, when she was publicly chastised by then-Prime Minister Goh Chok Tong and other Cabinet ministers for criticising the government for losing the moral authority to govern after raising their own ministerial salaries significantly. Lim's reach could only have been boosted when her novella *Leap of Love* was made into the movie *The Leap Years* by the Singapore film company Raintree Pictures. The romantic drama was screened at events such as the explorASIAN Festival in Vancouver, Canada,[14] representing the best of Singapore cinema. Lim's books – those published and distributed overseas – have probably been the most influential international literary contribution to nation branding for Singapore, going by the sheer number of readers.

Like Lim, there are other Singaporean authors whose works have also been published internationally, such as Gopal Baratham's novels *A Candle or the Sun* and *Moonrise, Sunset*, published by Serpent's Tail, and Hwee Hwee Tan's novel, *Mammon Inc*, published by Penguin, both in Britain as well. More recently, writers such as Ovidia Yu, Adeline Foo and Amanda Lee Koe have also reached wider audiences with publication and distribution overseas. Aside from novels, there have also been cross-cultural poetry anthologies such as *Writing Singapore*[15] and works by influential poets such as Edwin Thumboo that have reached more selected regional and international audiences, but the typically small readership for verse and for the literature of such a small country limits their direct impact on nation branding.

Once in a while, a book from, and about, Singapore manages to get significant attention internationally. Of the graphic novel *The Art of Charlie Chan Hock Chye* by Sonny

Liew, which won three Eisner awards in 2017, a review in 2016 by National Public Radio in the USA says the book "feels like Singapore between two covers. The pressure-cooker country – tiny and polyglot, globally competitive and politically repressive – seems to have been poured into this dense book."[16] As expected, some widespread perceptions of Singapore are summed up in that one passage. It will take many more such books to flesh out the true character of Singapore and its people and society.

Crazy Rich Asians and the real Singapore

Kevin Kwan's 2013 novel *Crazy Rich Asians* was a runaway bestseller for the Singapore-born writer who moved to the US in his teens. But it was the 2018 Hollywood movie of the same title, based on the book, that really moved the needle in global brand affinity for Singapore and put the island into the big-time on the world map. The smash romantic comedy, about the lives of Singapore's affluent elite, gained for the island countless mentions and references internationally in mainstream and social media. Tourists from everywhere yearned to visit the places featured onscreen, from the swanky Raffles Hotel to the smoky Newton Hawker Centre.

More importantly, keen interest in this movie phenomenon also led many to learn more about this former British colony, and this boosted its brand awareness even further. They were curious about the backstory of the sixth most millionaire-dense country in the world and the top across Asia (one in 34 people, according to data firm WealthInsight). *Time* magazine observed that "Singapore's determination to attract immigrants endures today, with alluring factors such as a low tax rate, a stable and safe government and a well-regulated banking system proving particularly tempting for wealthy people and businesses seeking a foothold in Asia".[17]

At the same time, how Singapore's public policies help sustain an unusually stable society is even more intriguing because they are so interventionist. *The Atlantic* magazine advised: "If you're an advocate for ethnic minorities, continually battling for every advance, Singapore's proactive approach [to race relations] can look like a dream come true – crazy woke. But we should be careful what we wish for. Here's the critical difference: Singapore's program of ethnic management isn't about accommodation; it's closer to entrenchment."[18]

As soon as the movie's trailer was released, debate surfaced in Singapore, suggesting that this society is not as "crazy woke" as *The Atlantic*'s writer imagined. Social commentators complained about the movie's poor representation of the Indian, Malay and other minorities of Singapore. Naturally, a film made from, and for, an Asian-American perspective cannot be expected to also include meaningful depictions of non-Chinese minorities in a totally different foreign society. So, yes, this movie stops short of reflecting Singapore's true multiracialism, which is a pity when this is, in fact, the main X factor of its country brand.

But this minor controversy also highlighted a deeper aspect of brand Singapore. In places like the US, marginalisation of Asian minorities in popular culture might persist more than they should, because Asian immigrants are insignificantly few, or have become resigned to languishing on the sidelines in more segmented societies. By contrast, the way that *Crazy Rich Asians'* treatment of racial minorities was queried in Singapore is perhaps a feature of a shared Singaporean aspiration towards inclusiveness, a sign of a more integrated society accustomed to multi-ethnic representation as a norm, and so, always expecting to see this diversity portrayed.[19] And so, even as people around the world began hankering to relive in reality the glitz and glamour of the movie's major scenes, among Singaporeans, a sharper clarity was forming about the true status quo of racial harmony.

Canvas for nation branding

As an art form, literature may be more enduring, but the visual arts are, for most people, the most accessible and arresting. The impact of painting and sculpture on nation branding is often underestimated, as it is easy to take for granted that, for most tourists and travellers to foreign countries, the visual arts provide the only significant interaction and engagement giving them an artistic sense of that place. Most travellers to a city would try to include at least a nip into a museum into their packed itineraries, although far fewer would buy a local novel at the airport on the way home. For Singapore, painting is the art form that has produced the most material for the projection of soft power, compared with the other visual art forms such as sculpture (where Ng Eng Teng was a notable name in earlier decades) or pottery (Iskandar Jalil), or other forms such as performance art. The Singapore Biennale, an islandwide contemporary art exhibition, was launched in 2006 and has become a platform event that puts Singapore on the world map of the visual arts. The first year was possibly the most momentous – 10 weeks, 95 artists and 19 exhibition venues, including some memorable ones such as a Hindu temple and a Catholic church.

At the same time, Singaporeans are making a mark in other events overseas. Ming Wong, a multi-disciplinary artist, received a Special Mention at the 2009 Venice Biennale, an event which some regard as "the Olympics of the visual arts scene" and is now a regular platform for nation branding through Singapore's design achievements. Wong presented a work titled *The Life of Imitation*, based on the golden era of Singapore's multi-ethnic film industry in the 1950s and '60s.[20] Going forward, the challenge is to keep up the power of attracting international attention as well as making artistic statements that can endure as much as they engage.

Other layers of Singapore's history sit waiting in the wings for further opportunities for subversion of international misperceptions of Singapore as a place with an uninteresting cultural history. Indeed, the visual arts – usually a most placid art form here – has previously depicted Singapore as a hotbed of political and social upheaval with regular worker strikes, student protests and race riots. An exhibition in 2007 at the Singapore Art Museum brought to life this period known as the time of "Malayan emergency", a term used by the British colonial government to describe its guerrilla war with the Malayan Communist Party in the 1950s, a dark, rather neglected period of Singapore's history.[21] In this exhibition, artworks by the then British-backed Singapore Art Society depicted a gentle life in the tropics, where fishermen and farmers went about their tasks peacefully (for example, Liu Kang's painting *The Padang* shows a lone figure maintaining the grass in front of the Supreme Court and City Hall – symbols of the British authority's orderliness), while across the gallery the social-realist Equator Art Society's paintings reflected the much grittier experiences of the local population, seeking to awaken a Malayan consciousness in the hope of forging the spirit of independence.

Fast forward to more recent times, and in painting, as with theatre and literature, only a few names stand out from the rest. Artists such as Thomas Yeo have won awards overseas, but the most prolific is watercolourist Ong Kim Seng, who has won several awards since 1983 from the American Watercolor Society including the 2000 Dolphin Fellowship.[22] Ong is the first Asian living outside the US to receive the rare honour, joining a prestigious group of more than 50 others who have become fellows since the 134-year-old society established the award in 1978 to promote excellence. Ong claims among his high-profile fans collectors including Queen Elizabeth II, former United Nations secretary-general Kofi Annan and former Indian prime minister Atal Bihari Vajpayee.[23]

An immense opportunity for nation branding that Singapore has yet to exploit is to properly showcase the nation's pioneer artists. A fuller platform than the existing Singapore Art Museum is now available in the form of the National Gallery Singapore,[24] which opened in 2015, an excellent example of adaptive reuse of the buildings of the former City Hall and Supreme Court. Only with a showcase of sufficient scale can pioneers such as the masters of the Nanyang School be presented to the world. This style of painting emerged in 1952, when the Singapore-based artists Liu Kang, Chen Chong Swee, Chen Wen Hsi and Cheong Soo Pieng went on their historic field trip to Bali.[25] These pioneer artists went to the Indonesian island mainly to search for a visual expression that was Southeast Asian. Not only did Bali offer them a rich visual source, the Balinese experience also revealed the ritualistic, experiential and decorative nature of Southeast Asian art – a point which sets the Singapore story apart from the exotic island influence of the 19th-century French Post-Impressionist painter Paul Gauguin, who found exotic inspiration on the Pacific islands of Tahiti, French Polynesia. The National Gallery has already contributed much to take Singapore's nation branding to a whole new level. Not only can it overturn misperceptions of Singapore's lack of soul, history and depth in the arts, but it could also convey the republic's admirable role as a custodian of some of the best artworks of Southeast Asia and Asia – a form of national "giving" to the world on behalf of the region that could add much to the nation's soft power.

New ways to score

Music is another field that has seen Singaporeans representing their country well overseas, from classical music performers such as pianists Seow Yit Kin and Margaret Leng Tan, violinist Siow Lee Chin and conductor Kahchun Wong, to contemporary musicians and singers such as Dick Lee and Stefanie Sun. Dick Lee deserves special mention for his works ever since his album *The Mad Chinaman* – a multicultural album with Indian *tabla* rhythms, Chinese *erhu* strings and Singlish sounds from the Malay song *Rasa Sayang* – shot him to fame in Japan.[26]

Sun joins a list of several other singers such as Kit Chan who have, in recent years, added more directly to internal nation branding with their performances of songs commissioned for the annual National Day Parade. While the achievements of these musicians cannot be denied, their specific contributions to nation branding have been mostly sporadic and more symbolic than substantive, and their audiences either mostly domestic or limited overseas. To use a musical metaphor, while Singaporean musicians add cadence and rhythm to the score of the Singapore branding symphony, it is the "lyrics" (as a metaphor for other forms of art and media) that can really add meaning and material to nation branding.

In the world of sports, Singapore made headlines at the 2008 Summer Olympic Games in Beijing, winning the team silver medal for table tennis. It was the nation's first Olympic medal in 48 years since Tan Howe Liang took a silver in weightlifting at the Rome Olympics in 1960. Despite drawing some criticism of Singapore's foreign-sports-talent scheme – from within Singapore as well as in China – the women's team, featuring new Singaporeans in former China nationals such as Feng Tianwei, grabbed more attention than other Singaporeans who have reached the pinnacle of their sports, such as former world bowling champion Remy Ong, who won the World Tenpin Bowling Championship at Busan in 2006.

But everything changed with the 2016 Olympic Games in Rio de Janeiro, when Joseph Schooling won Singapore's first-ever gold medal, in the process also setting a new world record in the 100 metres butterfly event and beating swimming legend Michael Phelps from the USA. No one can ever say again that Singapore is too small a country to produce an Olympic champion. Singapore also has a three-time gold medallist in Yip Pin Xiu for the backstroke event in swimming in the Paralympic Games, the Olympic Games for the physically disabled. Schooling, in particular, has been referenced countless times since in platforms that have some bearing on adding to the country brand, such as in the rousing finale of the *Bicentennial Experience* multimedia show in 2019.

"Track two" diplomacy in a "little red dot"

When it comes to individual Singaporeans who can play a part in contributing to building a country brand, those involved in the realm of what is called "track two diplomacy" are often at the forefront. These people are usually not officials in a formal appointment, but act in informal capacities in ways that can contribute much to build international relations, and, in the process, enhance their own country's brand.

For example, in their own ways, think-tanks such as the Institute of Southeast Asian Studies (ISEAS) have won friends and influenced many people on behalf of Singapore over the years. Much of what the ISEAS-Yusof Ishak Institute does is in the context of relatively small seminars, but the influence among thought leaders from around the region can be far-reaching behind these closed doors. The whole field of international relations, research and education has also been rich in potential for more positive input to Singapore's country brand.

In the 2000s, in a positive development for Singapore's nation branding, the assertive and divisive "Asian values" debate of the 1990s[27] was left behind for a more balanced argument for the world to pay greater heed to the rise of

Asia. Into the 2010s, the global balance has shifted yet again. The context for some of the international roles that Singapore used to play in the theatre of global public opinion has changed. For example, it used to be that Singapore could act as a kind of intermediary between "the West" and, say, China in the days when there was still vestigial meaning in the now very much dated term "bamboo curtain". This was when politicians from the Western world would look to "western-educated" Asian statesmen like Lee Kuan Yew to try and gain a deeper understanding of the "inscrutable East".

Today, the world has been transformed. Some Westerners now speak better Mandarin than many Asians. In mainland China, the command of English – often with an American accent – has taken a great leap forward. With direct lines of communication established with advancements in technology and globalisation, Singaporean public intellectuals on the international stage will have to work harder to have their voices heard. This could mean that the mindshare of brand Singapore might be diminished further in these spheres, unless effort is made to gain more influence on behalf of Singapore.

If the "tide" of Asian global influence rises, so too will Singapore's nation branding "boat" be lifted along with it. In the arena of international relations and diplomacy, the most outstanding Singaporean is, without doubt, veteran ambassador Tommy Koh, who served as Singapore's ambassador to the US and the UN, and as founding director of the Asia-Europe

Foundation. He has on countless occasions chaired and spoken at international forums, earning much brand affinity and equity for Singapore by often speaking from his own perspective and not as a government official.[28] His many achievements in elevating Singapore's standing on the world stage include his pivotal role in environmental diplomacy as President of the Third United Nations Conference on the Law of the Sea 1980–1982, establishing new concepts of international law such as exclusive economic zones and the common heritage of mankind. Professor Koh's book, *The Little Red Dot*,[29] illustrates his tireless efforts to enhance Singapore's nation branding. The book title joins in the rebranding by Singaporeans of the term attributed in 1998 to former Indonesian president B.J. Habibie about Singapore being just "a little red dot" on the world map. Koh's Foreign Ministry colleague, Professor Kishore Mahbubani, founding dean of the Lee Kuan Yew School of Public Policy, has also been very active as a voice of Asia in the intellectual space extending outside academia into public life as a commentator on issues such as the most important geopolitical issue today – relations between the US and China.[30] Other Singapore-based academics have also added to nation brand-building with their scholarship and engagement in public discourse, notably Professor Wang Gungwu of the National University of Singapore, an expert on the global Chinese diaspora.

Top institutions setting up campuses in Singapore contribute to enlargement of this potential, drawing on the country's attractive location for education in Asia, with examples such as the French global management school INSEAD. Singapore-based institutions have also boosted their value-add for nation branding by strengthening their linkages with top faculty and schools, such as Harvard Business School professor Michael E. Porter serving as chairman of the International Advisory Panel of the Asia Competitiveness Institute at the Lee Kuan Yew School of Public Policy, National University of Singapore,[31] and former UN Secretary-General and Nobel Peace Prize laureate Kofi Annan joining the Lee Kuan Yew School as the first Li Ka Shing Professor.[32] The untapped potential for nation branding in this sphere is the large number of other academics working in Singapore, including those from other countries, who could become much more active in public discourse to enrich the intellectual life of a country whose level of public discussion is generally not in sync with its socio-economic development.

Civil society has also begun in recent years to assert itself more, ranging from advances in environmental conservation by non-government organisations such as the Nature Society (Singapore) to assistance efforts in the region from NGOs such as Mercy Relief and Habitat for Humanity. In the space of environmental conservation, led by the Ministry of the Environment and Water Resources (reorganised into the Ministry of Sustainability and the Environment in 2020), Singapore's efforts in initiatives such as Pulau Semakau – where the island was developed into a long-term landfill that also served as a wildlife retreat, drawing visitors from afar – are winning more international recognition. Regional assistance initiatives such as during the 2004 Asian tsunami are similarly helping to enhance the country brand. In the wake of the disaster, the Singapore Red Cross and the Tsunami Reconstruction Facilitation Committee managed the Tidal Waves Asia Fund, implementing more than 70 projects on healthcare, education, housing and community, and economic recovery and livelihood in Indonesia, Sri Lanka and the Maldives.[33]

These "track two" contributions deserve to be better known beyond their respective spheres. Unfortunately, the reality remains that one filmmaker can potentially make a greater difference to nation branding than thousands of volunteers and donors. Still, something that can capture the imagination of mass audiences will add truly substantial and enduring input to how a nation is perceived and branded. Often, that contribution is best coming from an individual who has no institutional agenda or obligation, and so, is well-placed to offer the kind of branding that works best: something that is as authentic as it is authoritative.

From "cultural desert" to "cultural dessert"

It used to be that Singapore was too obviously more about hardware than software. Just 20 years ago, it was referred to disparagingly by its own people as well as outsiders as a "cultural desert". It used to be that you could attend every significant arts event in town – because there were so few. Today, the arts calendar is so full that, for a long time now, it has become humanly impossible to see every show that is on. Singapore has now even been termed a "cultural dessert",[34] to signal the paradigm shift that needs to be adequately considered by any commentator today on Singapore's nation branding. In recent years, Singapore has added significantly to its software as well. One of its most visible icons is its national performing arts centre, the Esplanade – Theatres on the Bay, affectionately called "the Durians" by Singaporeans because the domes that house its two performance halls resemble the shells of the spiky local fruit.

Most of these changes have come about as a result of a series of national initiatives to build – and to brand – Singapore as a "Renaissance city" and a "global city for the arts". As a national strategy to boost the arts, the republic went through three phases of its Renaissance City Plan[35] and more, with the latest blueprint being the Our SG Arts Plan, covering 2018 to 2022. These enhancements will transform the country's civic district into a world-class cultural and entertainment district with diverse arts and cultural offerings, especially with the National Gallery Singapore. With all this planning, investment and support, the house that is Singapore is "softening" by the day, being filled even more with the sound of music and the beauty of art. An unusually branding-activist public sector perseveres with its concerted, centrally planned series of nation branding and rebranding initiatives revolving around the arts. The private sector tries to add value to nation branding, sometimes indirectly or unwittingly. Ultimately, the voices of the people make the most crucial impact in representing the country in culture and other fields of expertise.

All in all, a unique picture of nation branding emerges – of a nation so tiny, yet so tenacious, in its desire to project itself on the world stage, so coordinated in its sustained cycles of self-positioning in its sub-brands, and yet so much subjected to the vagaries of foreign impression. Such are the challenges of nation branding, and the effort needed to marshal the wealth of meaning, not to mention the subconscious power of myth – something the next chapter examines in more detail.

CHAPTER 5

HEAR THE
LION ROAR

Myth, the Merlion and Singapore's regal brand

A T THE DAZZLING, high-tech opening ceremony of the world's first Youth Olympic Games[1] in
Singapore on 14 August 2010, three larger-than-
life characters dominated the stage: a dragon, a
phoenix and a massive technicolour monster representing a
demon of self-doubt. The third is a fantastical figment of the
imagination conjured to evoke its opposite – the key message of confidence – while the first two are the most iconic
symbols from traditional Chinese culture. In a way, it was a
missed opportunity to place on the platform a uniquely Singaporean brand ambassador such as the lion, after which the

Lion City is named. Of course, both the lion and the Merlion were present throughout the competition, in the form of the Singapore Games' mascots Lyo and Merly, but these two variations on the lion symbol were missing from the main show items.

Perhaps rightly, in the end, the designers of the opening show opted for imagery that contained a deeper cultural authenticity and wider appeal – two figures adapted from millennia-old creatures of Chinese legend and a third from the most modern international milieu of video games, a world in which many young people are known to spend much of their free time. Nonetheless, the absence of the lion and other Singaporean symbols is revealing. In a nutshell, it demonstrates the ambivalent position of national emblems generally in the nation branding of Singapore. Lyo and Merly might have appeared in the event's promotional materials, but when it came to something like the main show, the tendency was still to appeal to symbols that audiences would find recognisable and feel comfortable with, a status that the Merlion has yet to attain in global perception.

The Youth Olympic Games in 2010 can be seen as Singapore's version of a "junior coming-out party" on the world stage. The event was held on a much smaller scale than the 2008 summer Olympic Games in Beijing, of course, but it was no less significant to the hosts in nation branding terms. The Youth Olympic Games was Singapore's most important international gesture of nation branding to the sporting world. It was seen by those in government as a sign that the country had "arrived" on the world stage. Some believe that this was, in all likelihood, Singapore's once-in-a-lifetime chance to host an Olympic Games, given the size of the country. And there is no escaping this constraint, unless Singapore co-hosts a future event with one or more neighbouring countries. For instance, it was announced in 2019 that Singapore is part of a five-nation Asean bid for the 2034 football World Cup, together with Thailand, Indonesia, Malaysia and Vietnam.

In the international game of nation branding, Singapore can be said to start off already with a huge disadvantage. Most people see Singapore as a country with a double handicap – hemmed in by its small size, hampered by a short history. This mindset is framed from the starting-point of Singapore's independence in 1965. But this applies only within the terms of reference of national sovereignty, a concept of nation-states that is relatively recent in the history of mankind, with most theorists seeing it emerging as a 19th-century European phenomenon. In fact, in thinking about nation branding, it would be fruitful to include as much as is relevant from the history of that territory, stretching as far back as possible. This longer perspective of history became a norm only after 2019, the year of the Singapore Bicentennial. Alongside the commemoration of 200 years since the British colonialists first arrived, the Singapore government decided to encourage Singaporeans to delve even further back in time, and deeper, into the island's ancient history, all the way back to 700 years ago.

Mining Singapore's history

By way of comparative illustration, if one wanted to think in a comprehensive way about the nation branding of America, one would not only start from the Declaration of Independence in 1776 but go further back to include the history of the earliest Wild West settlers, the whole saga of slavery and the early lives of the native Americans. In other words, to catch all the "fish" relevant to nation branding, one should cast one's "net" over wherever and whenever any significant event or idea contributes to the present projected meaning and received understanding of that country brand. It could even be argued that one should also go beyond human history and include natural history – as in the history of plants, animals and even minerals – if any of these added to the current composition of the country brand. For example, in any study of the nation branding of Canada, it would be useful to include consideration of the botanical, agricultural and cultural history of the maple leaf, in all its relevant representations.

Applying this way of thinking to Singapore, one must go back in time way before 1965, back at least to the 13th century and to one of the first important figures of Singapore – Sang Nila Utama, who, according to legend, was the founder of ancient Singapore. He was a prince from Palembang, capital of the ancient Srivijaya empire, part of Indonesia today. The prince ruled the island from 1299 to 1347, according to the *Sejarah Melayu*[2] or *Malay Annals*, a literary work in the

Malay language that was commissioned in 1612 and chron-
icles the genealogies of the Malay rulers over 600 years in
the area that is today Malaysia and Indonesia. At that time,
the island that is today Singapore was a fishing village called
Temasek – "sea town" in the Javanese language. The earliest
written mention of Singapore is in a Chinese account from
the third century which refers to the island as "Puluozhong",
or "island at the end of the peninsula".[3] Archaeological exca-
vations have also unearthed evidence of human habitation,
with references to Singapore's ancient history as a regional
trade centre and much more than a maritime "pit-stop" along
the aquatic trade link called the Silk Route, which connected
China to the West for supply chain management for com-
modities such as silk, spices and sandalwood.

Legend has it that Sang Nila Utama, eager to identify
new territory for a new city and armed with what appeared
to have been imperialistic ambitions, decided to explore the
islands off the coast of Palembang. He set sail in a number
of ships and reached Temasek. The story is that, en route,
the ships encountered a great storm, and were faced with the
danger of sinking until the prince, on the advice of a ship's
officer, cast his heavy crown into the waters, whereupon
the tempest finally died down. Landing at the mouth of the
present-day Singapore River, the party went hunting in the
forest. It was then that the prince spotted a strange animal
with a red body, black head and white breast. It was a handsome creature that moved impressively back into the jungle.

Sang Nila Utama enquired of one of his chief ministers what animal it was, and was told it probably was a lion.

The way the story is told suggests an element of artistic licence, full of storytelling devices that are typical of myth and legend. And true enough, ever since, science has contradicted art. Studies of Singapore have indicated that lions have never existed on the island, not even Asiatic lions. Hence, some believe that the beast observed by Sang Nila Utama was more likely a tiger, probably the Malayan tiger. Others animals have also been suggested, including the golden cat or masked palm civet.[4] In any case, the prince saw this animal sighting as an omen of good fortune, and so, stayed on and founded a city. He named the city Singapura. "Singa" means lion and "pura" means city in the Sanskrit language; the name thus means "Lion City". Sang Nila Utama ruled Singapura for 48 years and is said to have been buried on what is today known as Fort Canning Hill.

The Lion King of Temasek

Some observers have suggested that the entire story of Sang Nila Utama is of doubtful authenticity, as some records show that the island was still called Temasek years later. Whether this is because the old name stuck for various reasons is unknown, due to the sketchiness of historical records from that era. Whatever the veracity, from the perspective of more recent history, there is no doubt that the legend of Sang Nila

Utama and the Singapura of that time have a secure place as part of the country's "early founding myths". Perhaps the lion-sighting story was never meant to be factual, but was a projection of symbolism, based on a fondness for the animal's suggestive power, as presented in the prince's own throne back home that was decorated with the figure of a lion, a popular symbol of power across many ancient civilisations. In this sense, in nation branding terms, perception truly *is* reality.

Thanks to Sang Nila Utama, the name "Lion City" has been used ever since for Singapore. A lion head emblem – a stylised red lion head in profile – is used to represent the country by the Singaporean civil service on many platforms, such as all government websites. As part of the National Day Parade 2020, the first parade since 1966 that was partially virtual, goodie bags were distributed to the public, with items including a face mask with this lion head emblem and the word "Singapore" printed on one side. More fanciful variations of the king of the jungle have emerged since 1965. Singa, a cartoon lion character, has been the ambassador of the country's courtesy campaign for decades. The National Courtesy Campaign was launched in 1979 by the then Ministry of Culture to help create a more pleasant social environment in a country in which a large proportion of the resident population were descended from migrant forefathers brought up in rural or urban blue-collar lifestyles.[5] The cartoon tradition has continued elsewhere, with one of the lion's most recent new incarnations being the mascot Lyo (incorporating into the made-up name the first two letters of the acronym "YOG", as opposed to the more common spelling "Leo"), created for the Youth Olympic Games in August 2010. The other mascot, Merly, is a "Merlioness cub", with blue scales on its torso and four animal limbs, instead of a fish body and tail.

The Sang Nila Utama story is a vital part of the way that Singapore has been imagined ever since 1299. Consciously – and much more often, subconsciously – it has helped shape the "imagined community" on this island, as part of the country's internal branding that has been sustained into modern times. The US-based Irish theorist Benedict Anderson defined nation-states as "imagined communities" in his 1983 book *Imagined Communities: Reflections on the Origin and Spread of Nationalism*. The concept states that a nation is a community that is socially constructed, which is to say it is "imagined" by the people who perceive themselves as part of that group. Such a sense of community is very real precisely because of these shared acts of imagination. The members of this community, being so numerous and far apart from each other, will never meet most of their fellow members, and yet, the feelings of kinship and affinity are not any weaker because of that physical distance.

This truism of anonymity and relative isolation from others perhaps applies even more so in a small country like Singapore, where the imaginative "leap" required is much less, as, for instance, there is not even a rural-urban divide to speak of. Still, the need for such community to be fostered is arguably just as great, if one factors in the human tendency to retreat into one's private space in densely urban environments, as well as the comparatively low level of appreciation for, and activism in, civil society in Singapore. Typically, there is only limited depth in relationships with most other fellow Singaporeans, hence a "vertical community" dimension is lacking. Instead, a deep "horizontal comradeship" is created and sustained through the constant self-reinforcing communication of information about common interests, such as news of fellow countrymen participating in global events like the Youth Olympic Games. Magnified by the mass media in creating and disseminating meaning, such occasions then become even more important in contributing to nation branding.

Singapore's *Beowulf*

If we believe, with Benedict Anderson, that nations are "imagined communities", then the boundaries of these acts of imagination should also take in content that originates at the margins. This would include raw material generated further back in time. In this regard, the way that ancient legends and any kind of founding myths are treated becomes especially important. It is here that the Sang Nila Utama legend may have been "modernised" and positioned on a footing that may cause complications later on. The legend of Sang Nila

Utama, in many senses, is to Singapore what *Beowulf* is to the Anglo-Saxon Western world. But the similarity with the Old English epic poem, written sometime between the year 720 and 796, ends there. The greater difference is in how the whole concept of myth has been treated to date in Singapore. *Beowulf* has seeped deep into the Anglo-Saxon psyche, infusing its meaning into a long and rich literary tradition, and its continued relevance is exemplified right up to the 2007 film of the same name.

In Singapore, however, it can be argued that a proper engagement with the Sang Nila Utama legend has not yet happened, if what is meant by this is that artists, intellectuals and other content creators of cultural resources have yet to sufficiently process the original myth into something that connects more fully with modern audiences, something that not only places the legend onto the "pedestal" of an imagined community's most ancient memories, but also draws public attention to the "plaza" of shared common space, where these memories are experienced together, and so, become part of everyone's lives.

Already, even without such artistic and cultural engagement, the development of the Sang Nila Utama founding myth has been interfered with by more recent exercises of commercially creative licence. This "interference", it can be argued, has made the roots of the myth's contribution to the nation branding of Singapore even weaker than they could have been.

Commerce versus culture

Singapore's long-standing brand associations related to the lion were given a modern twist even before independence, with the creation of the fantastical figure of the Merlion. The emblem of a massive fish with a lion's head was designed by Fraser Brunner, a member of the then tourism board's souvenir committee and curator of the Van Kleef Aquarium, from whence possibly arose the first immersion of Sang Nila Utama's lion into a maritime context and its merging with the body of a fish in the fashion of a mermaid. The Merlion was used as the logo of the Singapore Tourism Board (then called the Singapore Tourist Promotion Board) from March 1964 to 1997. A statue of the Merlion was conceptualised by Kwan Sai Kheong, then the vice-chancellor of the University of Singapore, inspired by the world-famous Little Mermaid statue in Copenhagen, Denmark.[6] The Merlion statue was constructed between November 1971 and August 1972 by the late Singapore sculptor, Lim Nang Seng, and unveiled at its original location on the Singapore River in September 1972.

In the brand representation that is the Merlion, there is, for the most part, a mixing of legend with a commercial rather than cultural engagement. This has undoubtedly had some impact, at least subconsciously, on even the least intellectually inquisitive observer, hence its undeniably limiting effect on nation branding. Unfortunately, the meaning of the Merlion – essentially in its brand promise, attributes and preferred brand associations – has never been properly artic-ulated by the brand owners, who include not just the state, but also the corporate sector and the people.

Given this measure of murkiness in brand meaning, the Merlion as a statue – devoid of the authenticity of ancient tra-dition and art, but with its origins crafted from pure tourism marketing – would possibly already be problematic enough. The questions become even more intriguing when animation is added, and this was in place for several years at the tower-ing 37-metre-tall Merlion-replica lookout attraction on the tourist resort island of Sentosa. For some years in the past, as visitors to the Sentosa attraction waited for their turn to take an elevator to the top of the Merlion statue, they watched a film with live actors dramatising the Sang Nila Utama story, using special effects. The video exercised creative licence by having Sang Nila Utama encounter the Merlion as a fearsome creature during a storm, no doubt abiding by the formulaic narrative norm of requiring a villain for the hero to contend with, thus setting the stage for eventual triumph and a "feel-good" ending.

In this theme park treatment, tradition was conjoined with "creative fusion" in pursuit of tourism marketing, in a way that created content requiring triple layers of suspen-sion of disbelief. The first layer was the status of legend that already surrounds the Sang Nila Utama story, especially the sighting of an animal that was said to give rise to the original naming of Singapore, as myth-making is wont to do. The second layer revolved around the Merlion, a creature created only in recent times with an express economic purpose of tourism promotion. The most problematic was the third layer of this video – the complication of merging the Sang Nila Utama story with a highly dramatised version of the Merlion that also added elements of menace and superstition, for purely commercial ends.

These somewhat negative traits conflicted with the otherwise benign sentiments exuded by the original Merlion at the Singapore River, as well as by the other Merlion replicas on the main island, including the one at Mount Faber. In recent years, the Sentosa video was replaced with an animated feature that was closer to the story in the *Malay Annals*, but with at least another two instances of creative licence. First, the lion that Sang Nila Utama spots was presented not as having a black head and red body, but as having "normal" lion colours and a face that reminded one of the Disney cartoon character, the Lion King. Second, the Merlion was represented as a purveyor of good luck, swimming in the sea together with two "Mercubs", with its less spectacular origins as a civil servant's invention glossed over conveniently, and probably leaving viewers puzzled about this.

It is intriguing to speculate what are the kinds of impressions and perceptions that tourists and other visitors might have taken away with them after watching this video of the stylised story merging the legend of Sang Nila Utama that is at least rooted in ancient literature with the entirely fictional narrative of the Merlion. There is not enough other supporting material – certainly not at the site itself – for visitors to do the work of separating fact and fiction. As all practitioners of branding know, one of the key success factors of branding is brand consistency. In any case, any impact that this inconsistency of presentation of the Merlion might have had on the overall brand-making of Singapore is now consigned to history, with the closure of this exhibit, announced in 2019, to make way for a makeover for Sentosa to enhance its tourism offerings further.

The Merlion in Singapore literature

The play with the Merlion myth is further extended into other spheres, including that of Singapore literature. Although the immediate readership of books of literature may be limited, literature possesses a tremendously enduring impact on the making of cultural references, and therefore of brand value, over time. Many Singapore poets have published poems about the Merlion. The best example is Singaporean poet Edwin Thumboo's seminal poem, *Ulysses by the Merlion* (1979), which is also engraved on a plaque beside the original Merlion statue now standing at Marina Bay, at the mouth of the Singapore River. In the poem, the poet introduces to Singapore another mythical element and dimension – citing the archetypal Western myth of the hero-explorer Ulysses. This sets up an interaction between ancient Greek and modern

Singaporean myth-making that continues to intrigue literary critics. Thumboo exercises poetic licence with time travel and imagines Ulysses gazing upon the Merlion, setting up musings on the nature of Singapore and its "trade" with symbols. This is how the poem ends:

> *Perhaps having dealt in things,*
> *Surfeited on them,*
> *Their spirits yearn again for images,*
> *Adding to the dragon, phoenix,*
> *Garuda, naga, those horses of the sun,*
> *This lion of the sea,*
> *This image of themselves.*

In these lines, Thumboo alludes to the clash of commerce ("dealt in things") and over-commercialisation ("surfeited on them") with culture, as represented by the Merlion and a figure like Ulysses. The way that the people of Singapore are imagined to "yearn again for images" can be interpreted to refer to a kind of vacuum among Singaporeans in identifying with, and having ownership of, cultural meaning, and this creates a sense of loss and emptiness in self-identity. Indeed, this lack of certainty about the country's most dominant imagery of cultural identity may explain partly the underlying inferiority complex in terms of brand identity of the nation and its people, especially in the earlier years of nationhood.

In a way, this sums up the untapped potential that exists between the cultural resource that is the Sang Nila Utama story and the way that it has been used in places such as at the Merlion replica on Sentosa. This gap is itself reflective of one of the key brand attributes of Singapore – the relationship between commerce and culture, and how the first tends always to dominate the second. In all important aspects of public life, the mindsets and motivations in this "GDP city" that propel policy and practice are invariably dominated by commercial interests (almost everything, it seems, is geared to try to add to the nation's gross domestic product) rather than more intrinsic cultural considerations. By way of illustration, consider how this theme – the way commerce always dominates culture – is dealt with in my poem *Merlion: Strike One* from the anthology *Reflecting on the Merlion: An Anthology of Poems* (2009). This is the sonnet's closing stanza:[7]

> lightning can strike twice, the powers-that-be grant,
> making this higher risk appetite extravagant:
> official rarity of form trumping function,
> swiftly-repaired mane left raring to restore,
> as you spew to the wind all caution,
> all-fixed symbol for another new Singapore

This poem refers to the incident of the Merlion statue at the Singapore River being struck by lightning in 2009 and suffering some damage on its head. This news was reported by wire agencies as far away as Azerbaijan, as the poem's epigraph notes. At that time, the authorities debated whether to install a lightning rod on the top of the Merlion's head to prevent a future strike but opted to take a chance on this and leave the Merlion without such a rod, and so, not spoil the statue's elegant look. This instance of "form trumping function" is seen in the poem as an "official rarity", an uncharacteristic case of officialdom preferring to permit prettiness to precede pragmatism.

The loosening-up of rules in more and more sectors of life in Singapore has been a feature since the 1990s and into the start of the 21st century. Hence, the difference in thematic focus from the time of the poem *Ulysses by the Merlion* to the more sophisticated world of *Merlion: Strike One* encapsulates the evolution of the primary concerns of Singapore society in that period, from the emphasis at the time of the first poem on the hardware for trade and the search for national identity ("this image of themselves") to a greater appreciation in the period of the second poem of the software for tourism, national reinvention and nation branding ("another new Singapore").

A royal heritage

Sang Nila Utama and Ulysses aside, by and large, thinking about brand Singapore has been mostly confined to the republic's most recent history as an independent nation, even though there is a period of some 700 years earlier to draw from. The result is that most discussion of the nation branding of Singapore was previously focused only on a narrow period of the five decades or so since 1965. Among the worst-case scenarios emerging from this is the conclusion that one should therefore not bother to even think too much about a country brand for Singapore since it is so new and undeveloped, and lacks material to work with. This inhibiting factor is a very serious one, because it impacts on – and, in a few ways, impairs – the development of the country brand henceforth and in every other way.

What is the sum-total effect of having a country brand whose origins are steeped in the legend of a figure like Sang Nila Utama and how the country came to be called the Lion City? The earliest name associations revolve around notions of grandeur and royalty, including the fact that Sang Nila Utama himself was a prince. The lion is universally revered as the king of the animals and is a symbol of royalty in many other countries, including those with strong branding such as Britain with its "three lions" emblem. The British lion's influence on its former colony Singapore is seen in other ways as well, for instance in how the "Kallang Roar", the din created by a full house of fans at Singapore's old National Stadium, was originally derived from the "Wembley Roar" at Britain's national stadium in London.[8]

On balance, however, it would seem that there has been comparatively less emphasis on the group of "macho" elements embedded in Singapore's use of lion brand associations. The masculine aspects of the lion are projected on such platforms as the state crest and other symbols of government such as the crest of the Singapore Armed Forces. Given the pervasive and powerful authority of the state in the making of Singapore's country brand, these depictions have more than carried their weight of influence over the decades. However, even in the more serious-minded lion head emblem used by the government on its online and print representations, any louder associations with strength and aggression are generally toned down, in favour of more subdued, subtler messaging.

Hence, there is a sense of dignity rather than daring, fortitude in place of ferocity. From Singa the smiley courtesy-campaign lion to Lyo the prancing Youth Olympic Games mascot, what has been just as prominently projected both internationally and to domestic audiences are the lion's more feminine and child-like characteristics. In this regard, the Merlion itself is an example of a curious gender inversion, creating a quite masculine adaptation of a well-known, intensely feminine figure of the mermaid from European folklore in a merger with a lion, the most macho of animals. The femininity of a mermaid weaves in an underlying strand of gentle timidity in the history of Singapore's nation branding, something that one could argue is somewhat at odds with typical brand associations surrounding the idea of the king of the jungle, the lion.

In 2019, the announcement came as a surprise that the Merlion on Sentosa, which had stood for 24 years, was slated to be demolished.[9] This will be part of the island's projected redevelopment to cater to a forecasted boost in tourism arrivals, a plan that was later slowed down by the Covid-19 pandemic. That a Merlion could be removed just like that speaks to a pragmatism that is typical of Singapore. However, this is an "auxiliary" statue, that does not possess the sacred status of the original Merlion at the Singapore River. In any case, what matters is the essence of the symbol, not just the physical form – the abstract idea, not even the concrete representation.

Singapore's national animal, or lack thereof

With no real-life "challenger", the lion has filled in the vacant role of Singapore's "physical" national animal. This happened because most Singaporeans are aware that lions have never existed on the island, but have never really thought about having an actual national animal. The tiger also appears on the state crest, but it belongs to the Malaya of the past and to Malaysia today, and so, cannot qualify as a national animal. For some reason, Singapore's first government in 1965 named a national flower – the orchid hybrid Papilionanthe Miss Joaquim – and then stopped short of naming any other national species, including a national tree, like the maple of Canada or the cherry blossom of Japan. As for a national bird, the crimson sunbird was proclaimed as such in 2015 by the Nature Society (Singapore) after a public poll, but this does not count, as it was not officially recognised.

Many countries celebrate their official national animals, such as Australia's kangaroo and China's panda. Images of these creatures appear everywhere, from flags to fridge magnets, seared into the subconscious, practically influencing, if only subconsciously, every citizen's thought, word and deed. Citizens of these nations draw much national pride and self-confidence from brand attributes such as power and grace that these animals represent, or from the brand affinity – and hence, goodwill – that they know people around the world feel, simply from familiarity with these national animals. Somehow, this is the deeply invaluable effect of having a national species to be inspired by – it is like a kind of life-force, an endless reservoir of character, from which citizens can draw spiritual sustenance.

Whereas US citizens can speak to foreigners at length about the spirit of independence of their American bald eagle, and American nature-lovers can elaborate on many other native species, the average Singaporean would be hard-put to say much about Singapore's wild animals. This is a pity, as the island's biodiversity is actually very rich, with many species of interest, from the Sunda pangolin to the Malayan colugo. Most Singaporeans remain unaware of Singapore's endemic species, including the three known endemic crabs such as the *Johora singaporensis*, a critically endangered freshwater crab that grows up to only one inch wide. The absence of a national animal results in a gap in internal brand-building, which probably exacerbated a policy neglect of wildlife in earlier decades, in contrast to the intensive nurturing of animals in captivity and the extensive resources devoted to cultivated gardens, inspired by the symbolism of the national flower.

Since the late 2010s, the smooth-coated otter has emerged as a strong contender for a national favourite animal. Drawn to urban Singapore by its cleaned-up waterways, the otter's popularity has been boosted by a growing general fondness among the citizenry for animals, as reflected in the sunrise industry of pet shops, and the sharing of many social media images of sightings of otter families frolicking across the island, even if these otters sometimes devour expensive koi fish in ornamental ponds. Nonetheless, without any other species being officially recognised, the lion remains the official "imaginary" national animal, depicted on the state crest and as a national symbol in various guises. With no real-life representation, this puts the lion of Singapore actually in the same category of mythical national animals, like the dragon of Bhutan and Wales.

The strand of "regal" branding surrounding the lion – and, partially, also the Merlion – could have been built on, and reinforced, much more over the years through official initiatives and being embraced by corporations and the people. Instead, the lion-related brand attributes of the Singapore brand have essentially been understated, even if the essential power of the lion symbol in itself has actually survived the softening, somewhat cartoonish, added characterisations over the years. Without strong internal anchors – which metaphors like national animals can offer – the trouble with nation branding is that any country brand can be buffeted by influences and perceptions from outside that are quite beyond the control of the brand owner, the home country. Some of these effects can be quite negative and leave enduring scars, as the next chapter will examine.

CHAPTER 6

ENOUGH TO CHEW ON?

Sticky stereotypes, "brand keloids" and brand recovery

S OME OF WHAT Singapore has invested in nation branding over the last few decades has actually been spent not on brand consolidation so much as on brand recovery. In other words, some of the additional input to the store, or score, of branding is mainly helping to close a deficit rather than to gain ground. This is mostly the fault of the "nanny". Over the years, some part of any advancement for Singapore's country brand in the international arena has been in recovering from the negative impact of the one name that has stuck especially until the 2000s:

"the nanny state", although this effect has declined since then. Indeed, Singapore had often been described as though it had sole claim on this epithet, despite other countries being at times even more fastidious in their "nannying duties". For instance, when the international media reported in 2006 on Singapore's move to open two casinos, the *New York Times* headline was: "The nanny state places a bet".[1] No further description or qualification needed. Just "the", not "a".

The "nanny state"

How did this come about? Singapore's "nanny state" reputation became deeply etched in the memory mainly after two incidents: the ban on the import and sale of chewing gum in 1992 (to prevent wastage of public resources cleaning up gum stuck on trains and in other public places) and the caning of American teenager Michael Fay for car vandalism in 1994 (to maintain social order). Such laws, seen as draconian through Western eyes, reflected Mr Lee Kuan Yew's determination since 1965 to make Singapore "a first-world oasis in a third-world region".[2] Thus, by this reckoning, any brand deficit that the nation still faces can be said to have been partly self-inflicted.

The larger backdrop to this brand deficit covers an overall approach to governance that has been in force throughout the republic's independent history, stretching back to include many other episodes such as those in media regulation – including the ban on *Cosmopolitan* magazine in 1982 for racy content – as well as the prohibition, in the business space, of things like casinos, bungee jumping and even neon lighting. There is the well-known story of how the Japanese New Age musician Kitaro was barred at immigration at Changi Airport from entering Singapore in 1985 because he had waist-length hair.[3] This was a leftover from an earlier era when men with long hair were associated with decadent "yellow culture" lifestyles considered socially undesirable. More broadly, the "nanny" instinct has also been seen to figure in various aspects of social engineering, ranging from government matchmaking for singles to reminding people to flush public toilets. As Mr Lee said in an interview in *The Straits Times* in 1987: "I say without the slightest remorse, that we wouldn't be here, we would not have made economic progress, if we had not intervened on very personal matters – who your neighbour is, how you live, the noise you make, how you spit, or what language you use. We decide what is right. Never mind what the people think."[4]

The media and "brand keloids"

The Kitaro incident would seem incredible now to a new generation born since the 1980s. In fact, the pendulum has swung all the way to the opposite side – someone like the Japanese musical genius would today be actively wooed to add to the "cultural vibrancy" of a country aiming to be a leading "Renaissance" global city well-known for its arts, culture and entertainment scene. But it must be remembered that asking a famous musician to have his hair cut at a national border or leave (what some might believe of a backward Third World territory) took place not too far back in memory – it was as recent as 1985 – while the two most far-reaching incidents adding to negative international branding – banning chewing gum and caning Michael Fay – happened even more recently, in the 1990s. This may go some way to explain why the negative stereotypes of Singapore have stuck as steadfastly as chewing gum.

Time, of course, can heal all wounds, but some scars become keloids and stay with you for life. Likewise, some deep negative branding perceptions can stick like what one might call "brand keloids". A real flesh keloid can be removed surgically, but it would be troublesome, cost a fair bit of money, and definitely be quite painful. In a similar way, a "brand keloid" cannot be easily excised. So entrenched is the term "nanny state" that attempts at variations of the nickname do not have much success, even if the writer is a noted one, such as Seth Mydans of *The New York Times*: "Sometimes called a nanny state for its smothering top-down control, Singapore might also be called a macho state, in which government warriors of social engineering and economic development command the citizenry."[5] The "macho" aspects of social control – the social engineering and the behind-the-scenes steering – evoke less obvious characteristics of a nanny and much more of another type, like an architect or engineer. But in the fight for negative branding dominance, the nanny, loaded with some sexist baggage as well, has beaten the macho male, hands down. Having such a "brand keloid" is what sets Singapore apart from a country like, say, Bhutan, which is universally associated with happiness, just as Singapore is perhaps best-known – if one had to pick just one attribute – for efficiency, as a place "where everything works". The big difference is that the mountain kingdom has no "brand keloids" to speak of.[6]

Some people might question whether the Lion City's major negative stereotypes have truly become "brand keloids". But, judging by the most recent inspection of the global landscape, the answer – unfortunately for Singapore – is "yes", at least for now. In a review of the Singapore-made movie *Sandcastle*, the British film critic Tony Rayns refers to Singapore as "an ultra-conformist nanny state".[7] The wire agency *Agence France-Presse* describes Singapore as having "a reputation as a nanny state that interferes in citizens' private lives [and] regularly carries out campaigns to instil discipline, promote courtesy and discourage the use of broken English... Other initiatives included a campaign urging wedding guests to arrive on time and rating public toilets for cleanliness."[8]

One major reason for such perceptions being affirmed is the extent to which the main national media in Singapore – both print and broadcast – is used on a daily basis for the government to speak to its own people. In such a media environment, much of this key messaging – what can be seen as a kind of dialogue "within the family" – is delivered essentially unfiltered. By using the mainstream media as the primary – and utterly pervasive – platform for such public communication, the government believes it achieves its communication aims in the most practical and efficient way. But a crucial side-effect is to be "eavesdropped" upon all the time by the rest of the world – with one of the consequences being the perpetuation of the "nanny state" image.

Thus, the international "nannifying effect" for Singapore is magnified manifold by the simple fact of the "educational role" that the mainstream media plays every day. This is also further magnified by the media's lack of room for manoeuvre to question the status quo. One could even suggest that this particular strand of negative branding adds to the self-inflicted reputational harm. By contrast, in some countries – including all those that have, or host, the "Western media" – the mass media is usually so unfriendly towards the government that any similarly "nanny"-style messages from the authorities would systematically be ignored or ridiculed on first delivery, or, at least, accompanied on first hearing with no-holds-barred critique and commentary. So, any such "nanny" characteristics in other countries – and there are many – would never even be conveyed.

The people as nanny

The situation is not helped by the willing acquiescence and support of the people themselves – indeed, the "nanny state" perception could hardly be sustained for so long if the circumstances were otherwise. This also explains the continuance of "behaviour modification campaigns" in many aspects of life, from speaking good English to dating. Even as some Singaporeans view such campaigns as somewhat overbearing and even condescending, they nonetheless go with the flow much more than they would put up anything resembling visible resistance. As Daryl Gan, a 29-year-old computer engineer in Singapore, was quoted saying, with a touch of sarcasm, in an *Associated Press* article in 2004: "The government does treat us like children sometimes, and they sweeten the deal with free gifts. It's our fault for buying it. We allow the government to tell us how to do everything... how to love, how to talk, how to adjust our watches."[9] The last item about time-keeping was a false example, for exaggerated effect, but such a situation is problematic because, if allowed to, social trends such as a more fundamentalist wave of social conservatism might try to take over the "nanny" role from the state, with possibly further-reaching consequences.

The cost of such negative branding as a nanny state is obvious, for example, if it is carried in a forum such as the Economist Intelligence Unit's country risk briefing, which goes out to potential investors and foreign talent who might wish to move their money or themselves to the republic. For instance, the EIU has suggested that "a paternalistic approach discourages individuals from participating in what some critics have described as a nanny state".[10] Although the specific context of the reference here is politics, the implied broader application is to curb initiative in other sectors as well, including those that have bearing on economics and business.

Sometimes, the fault of brand stereotype "scarring" truly lies on the side of the media. On occasion, the reference to a "nanny state" is simply superficial and tries too hard to sound sophisticated, producing instead the opposite effect. Take, for instance, this description from *Time Out* magazine of a visit to the Long Bar of the Raffles Hotel: "I go to Raffles Hotel, birthplace of the Singapore Sling, where the ambitiously priced cocktails are less of a draw than the old wood in the long bar and the right to throw peanut shells on the floor. Yes – this is the only place in Singapore where littering is allowed. My disproportionate glee at chucking shells reminds me of a toddler throwing food; this nanny state is infantilising me. I'd better get out before I'm rendered too docile to go."[11] Unfortunately, commentators who are "parachuted" in to write on Singapore sometimes take the easy way out and refer to old stereotypes plucked from a quick round of desktop research and then perpetuated with yet another repetition. What is infamous becomes even more infamous.

At other times, the intent is serious but no less off-the-mark. For instance, the *Financial Times*, referring to the two integrated resorts at Marina Bay and Sentosa, said they would "help the island shed its international image as a nanny state that jails people for chewing gum".[12] Imprisonment for just chewing gum, of course, is a factually inaccurate description one should not expect of a leading publication in the global financial media, even if, in this case, the writer was then relatively new to Singapore. Clearly, such instances demonstrate how old and deep are the "brand keloids" of negative branding that Singapore still has to recover from. And the old mindset has not gone away even today. For instance, a *New York Times* column in May 2020 about Singapore's handling of the Covid-19 pandemic noted that "the government had controlled a fearsome new disease with the same tools it used to control its residents: pragmatism, efficiency and extreme surveillance".[13] The impulse to overstate one's case is an occupational hazard familiar to any professional writer. Often, the urge to exaggerate also indicates some measure of ideological bias. Hence, any brand recovery effort will have to recognise such realities and work with and around them, rather than to try to wish them away or, worse still, confront them head-on – in other words, by using soft power, not hard power.

Indeed, this different, softer approach to criticism can now be seen in many ways. Whereas the Singapore government of an earlier era might have been tempted to take the international media to task for any criticism, an alternative response today would be to cajole rather than to clash, to tango rather than to tangle. This stance was articulated, for example, at a branding forum in 2007, when the minister for education then, Tharman Shanmugaratnam, said that Singapore should not be defensive or lose any sleep over being called a "nanny state" or other names.[14] Speaking at a Public Relations Academy conference, he acknowledged: "We are referred to affectionately as a nanny state… an overly sanitised city. A 'fine city', with penalties for numerous offences." Instead, Singapore should remember that every city develops its own buzz, he said, a mix of the good bits and the bad, and should build on the positives that enhance the country's image, including having a trusted system with good governance, and being the most open city in Asia. "Zurich does not try to be as exciting as Madrid or San Francisco. It has an interesting fringe culture, but it is by and large a very predictable city, even boring by some accounts. But it comes out near the top in many polls as a city that attracts talent, especially those with families." So, Singapore could take the nanny tag in its stride, and should mostly carry on doing its own thing, with its eyes on its long-term aims, whether it is to win investments or to woo talent.

The "911 effect"

More recently, the pendulum has swung in Singapore's favour in terms of the divide between more liberal and more conservative positions on a society's openness and flexibility with restraints.

In 2010, Swiss expatriate Oliver Fricker was found guilty of breaking into a train depot in Singapore and spray-painting graffiti across two carriages; he was sentenced to three strokes of a rattan cane and five months in prison – extended to seven months following an unsuccessful appeal.[15] The Swiss national found that his government accepted the punishment being meted out and would not protest in any way, unlike the way the US government appealed for clemency in 1994 for Michael Fay. During the time of the earlier episode, the ideological gap on civil liberties between Singapore and the US was like a "Grand Canyon", with the US then led by a Democrat president, Bill Clinton, who saw in the Fay issue an occasion to reaffirm American values. During the term of Barack Obama, with another Democrat in the White House, the attitude towards the preservation of order in society had become quite different in a changed world after the 911 terrorist attacks on New York City in 2001. Describing this new stance on civil liberties, Rahul Jacob of the *Financial Times* put it most starkly: "The world has changed and become more like Singapore... At some level, we are all Singaporeans now."[16]

Singapore's founding prime minister, Lee Kuan Yew – whom *The New York Times* once dubbed "the world's most eloquent autocrat" – had a long-running argument with the US about democracy and civil liberties. But, as Lee's son and prime minister since 2004, Lee Hsien Loong, told *Institutional Investor* in 2010: "They used to say, 'Why do you impose these limits? Why do you lock up people without trial?' That was before Guantanamo Bay... Now, perhaps, we are not as far apart."

The narrowing of this ideological gap will go quite some way to help Singapore in its brand recovery efforts. This outcome of the actions of a band of terrorists in the 911 attacks is perhaps a remarkable example of the far-reaching, hard-to-foresee impact of actions in a much more globalised world. The divide in political ideology has narrowed in other places as well. Jacob added in the same *Financial Times* article: "Even Hong Kong, which kidded itself about being everything that Singapore wasn't, has changed. Lawmakers in Hong Kong passed a bill in August [2006] allowing more covert surveillance of its citizens, including phone tapping and bugging homes, which the government says is necessary to combat crime."[17] Since then, events in Hong Kong have evolved even further down this path, especially after a new national security law was passed in 2020.

Learning from the nanny

The post-911 perspective, now further complicated by developments since Covid-19 changed the world, has also fostered a deeper appreciation of the need for, and benefits of, the characteristics of a nanny, such as close supervision deployed by the state to ensure public safety. In Singapore's case, the background goes as far back as the last racial riots in 1964 and continues right up to the recent rise of fundamentalist religion, radicalisation and associated violence. Singapore's uniquely interventionist measures include a whole social network closely managed by the state to ensure that no one and nothing risks jeopardising the country's fundamentals of meritocracy, secularism and multiracialism. This includes institutions such as the Presidential Council for Minority Rights, legislation such as the Religious Harmony Act, and regulations such as the ethnic quota scheme in public housing allocation to prevent the formation of racial enclaves.[18] Such ethnic harmony is, in itself, one of the best brand attributes of Singapore, and deserves to be more widely known.

Actually, being a nanny is not that much of a problem for everyone. Life is so compartmentalised that in the economic sphere, for example, being a "nanny state" has never been much of an issue at all. In most nation brand indexes, a factor like "ease of doing business" will typically carry more weight than, say, something like freedom of the press. This is why Singapore's low ranking on the Reporters Without Borders' world press freedom index – dropping seven places from the year before to an all-time low of 158th out of 179 countries in 2019 – does not pull down its overall country brand rankings when all factors are taken into account. In fact, one could almost say that a place at one hypothetical extreme position of media freedom – a country led by a benign and benevolent dictator – would, in many ways, be considered a best friend by foreign investors, because such a market system

could be more easily steered to benefit business interests. As
Rahul Jacob of the *Financial Times* put it: "Dubai, meanwhile,
rarely seems to have had an idea about economic development
it did not borrow from the Singapore model. A few years ago,
an unusual business-government partnership in Bangalore
said it wanted to make the city India's Singapore."

And if it used to be that developing countries would
make a beeline for Singapore to seek to unearth the "secrets"
of its success, it seems that, now, even the superpowers are
looking to learn what they can. For example, during the
Brexit debate in Britain around the referendum of 2016,
Brexiteers were calling for Britain to become a "Singapore-
on-the-Thames", what they saw (not entirely accurately) as a
low-tax, lightly regulated economy that can out-compete the
over-regulated eurozone.[19] Earlier, in 2003, London implemented its congestion charge for vehicles entering the central
part of the British capital after officials visited Singapore to
study the Electronic Road Pricing (ERP) scheme run by Singapore's Land Transport Authority. Launched by the Ministry
of Transport in 1998, the electronic toll-collection system is
the focus of daily complaint from citizens but is touted as an
example of public service innovation that has attracted attention around the world. A precursor to the ERP, a manual Area
Licensing Scheme around the central business district controlled by policemen and using tickets, was the world's first
congestion pricing system when it was started in 1975. Singapore also imposes vehicle quotas to control car ownership,

with vehicles requiring Certificates of Entitlement that buyers have to bid for, for up to tens of thousands of dollars each, to last just 10 years. This system is being adapted and replicated in the Chinese capital of Beijing, to curb its growing car population.[20]

In a 2009 article with an attention-grabbing headline, "What Singapore Can Teach the White House", William McGurn of *The Wall Street Journal* summed it up this way: "When it comes to healthcare, Uncle Sam has better claim to the nanny title."[21] Comparing the two healthcare systems during a time of intense debate in the US on healthcare reform, McGurn concluded: "Singapore's system isn't perfect. It does suggest, however, that the Average Joe stands more to gain from a system where hospitals and doctors compete for patients, where patients have different price options for their hospital stays and appointments, and where they pay for some of it out of pocket." "Nanny" is used here in a good way, to refer to the welfare approach of the US. What is clear, in terms of nation branding, is that "nanny", used on Singapore, is today much less of a sarcastic indictment, and is instead travelling further along on the road towards one day becoming a universal term of endearment and even of praise. Indeed, in a world devastated by Covid-19, a government that acts like a nanny to look after its citizens would be much preferred to one that left its people to fend for themselves.

"Reverse bungee" options

Meanwhile, if chewing gum had such a big role to play in creating Singapore's negative brand positioning in the first place, it would seem that the solution is not too far away. Lester Thurow, the renowned Massachusetts Institute of Technology management and economics professor, suggested lifting the ban on importing chewing gum in 2000, when policy-makers were all discussing what Singapore could do to attract talent from Silicon Valley and other sources of high-tech creativity, amid the then "dotcom boom" and the global euphoria over the "New Economy".[22] "Change the law on chewing gum, because it makes the rest of the world think you control everything, which you don't," he said. The joke about Singapore being a "fine" city with its many rules and penalties for anti-social behaviour had got so out of hand that apparently the American pop star Mariah Carey had asked, ahead of her trip, whether she would be arrested for wearing a bikini during her visit to Singapore in 2000.

It is true that perception can outlive reality. But at least after you do alter reality, misperception stands a better chance of change. "Brand keloids", like their real-life counterparts in scars on human flesh, may linger for life, but a strong brand personality can make observers forget that those "brand keloids" are even there, after some time has passed. For chewing gum, perceptions have already improved, and will continue to get better. It took nothing less than the

US-Singapore Free Trade Agreement that came into force in 2004 for the chewing gum import ban to finally be modified, if not removed. This came about after lobbying led by former US Representative Philip Crane of Illinois,[23] the US state that is home to chewing gum manufacturer Wrigley's. Gum import was re-allowed into Singapore, but only "therapeutic" gum meant for dental hygiene or as an anti-smoking aid.

In some other areas, there have been partial U-turns. For example, bungee jumping, long disallowed, is still not available. Instead, there is a "reverse bungee" ride at Clarke Quay by the Singapore River, where patrons are swung upwards into the air instead of flung down from a height. The reversal in direction reflects nonetheless the stance of the new Singapore, seemingly determined to turn its international image right side up, as it were, even if it means accepting compromises along the way. Other significant relaxations include the lifting in 2004 of the 22-year ban on *Cosmopolitan* magazine for its liberal content,[24] a follow-up to recommendations by the 2003 Censorship Review Committee, a citizens' panel formed to review media regulation policies periodically. That same year, the cable TV series *Sex and the City* was unbanned after five years, but there were still cuts when deemed necessary by the censors, despite cable TV being granted more leeway in content. In comparison, the 2010 Censorship Review Committee did not announce any similarly significant opening up, mainly because, by then, the impact of the Internet had made most of the restrictions of earlier years practically redundant. For instance, Singapore remains a country that has strict legal regulations on, for example, pornography in print or on video, but globally, pornography has moved almost entirely online anyway.

Other measures that opened up in a particular area but retained some limits include "allowing" homosexual employees in the public service[25] but retaining laws against homosexual sex. These are what might be called "reverse bungee" options – liberalisations that go only part of the way, or are modified to suit the perceived uniquely Singaporean context. In the case of censorship, a key future challenge will be whether the government continues to abide by its stated approach to move with the people, and not ahead of them.[26] Given the people's conditioned dominant default mode of followership, and the prevailing balance of political and moral conservatism, the question is whether such a cautious approach to media regulation is not at odds with other stated policy aims, as well as with recommendations of other panels such as the Economic Strategies Committee to foster a global city by giving the arts the space to nurture creativity and empowering a people to truly dare to dream and to do.

All this while, the missing piece of the jigsaw has been something crucial in branding – brand affinity, a feeling that draws the audience towards a brand, something that makes you want to be more closely associated with that brand. This may boil down to the difference between admiration and envy, as David Lamb, writing for *Smithsonian* magazine in

2007, put it: "[Singapore...] the 'perfect' society. Yet, perfection came at a price. Personal freedoms were surrendered, creativity and risk-taking never flourished, the leadership seemed to lurk behind every tree. Singapore was admired but not envied."[27] The question for now is whether Singapore can up the "envy factor" for foreign audiences – and this depends on whether the current and future phases of opening up will be confident and generous enough to foster such brand affinity. Another facet of the gap between perception and reality is that, while international journalists might not always envy Singapore, anecdotally, people who have moved to Singapore to work and live often express both admiration and envy for the city-state's positive aspects. Indeed, sometimes, expatriates are more enthusiastic than citizens in praising Singapore.

The "semi-permeable membrane"

The period of Singapore's modern history that saw, among other things, a stunning reversal on the previous ban on casinos was nothing less than a fundamental remaking and a new era. This is how the rationale was summed up by *Institutional Investor* magazine in 2006: "What was at stake, [Prime Minister Lee Hsien Loong] argued, was not morality, but survival. Singapore's share of Asian tourism arrivals had fallen from 8 per cent in 1998 to 6 per cent in 2002. By contrast, the former Portuguese colony of Macau, where gambling is the major attraction, was enjoying a boom. Last year, tourist arrivals to Macau swelled by 40 per cent, to 16.7 million – more than twice Singapore's 8.3 million. Other Asian countries are also looking to open or expand casinos, while Hong Kong is hoping to lure leisure travellers with a Disneyland theme park that opened last year. Unless Singapore could come up with its own attractions, it risked losing out in the world's fastest-growing tourism market."[28]

This broader about-turn, naturally, is being driven top-down. The new direction was signalled in 2004, a few months before Mr Lee took over as prime minister. In a speech at a Harvard Club of Singapore event, he said that it was time for the nation's long-ruling government to stop acting like a full-time nanny. "If we want a more participatory citizenry, the government will have [to] cut the apron strings and leave more matters to the private and people sectors. Nanny should not look after everything all the time."[29] This momentum has been maintained. For example, the Hyde Park-inspired Speakers' Corner at Hong Lim Park, set up in 2000, has been further relaxed, so that speakers can just register online with the parks board (a friendlier authority) and go and speak, whereas in the past they had to first get approval from the police.

If Singapore manages to reap the economic benefits of having two casinos while keeping at bay enough of the social ills that inevitably accompany gaming, it might succeed in creating a kind of new country sub-brand – a country that is able to absorb high-stakes gaming into its system and yet maintain a brand reputation for wholesomeness. The metaphor for this kind of filtering process is a scientific one, which is perhaps not surprising coming from Singapore's foreign minister, Vivian Balakrishnan, a medical doctor by training: "That's part of the secret to our success: maintaining this semi-permeable membrane. Make it permeable to success, impermeable to the unsavoury elements."[30]

In the first half of the 2010s, Singapore's international reputation suffered just a bit – a few knocks only in some quarters, such as the controversy over the initial state legal action in 2015 against Amos Yee, a teenaged YouTuber who attracted international attention for, among other things, a YouTube video criticising Lee Kuan Yew upon his death. By contrast, the decision in 2014 to restrict the public screening of *To Singapore With Love* – a movie directed by Tan Pin Pin, featuring interviews with former detainees living overseas in exile – for "national security" reasons did not attract as much of a reaction. In any case, the movie is now accessible online.

At home, new legislation such as those regulating news websites and on other aspects like contempt of court reined in some of the exuberance in online postings. Outside Singapore, in the larger scheme of things, episodes like the one involving Yee can now just come and go. They do not seem to stick like they did in the past, such as with the chewing gum import ban or the caning of the car vandal Michael Fay. In 1993, the science-fiction writer William Gibson caused a stir with his *Wired* magazine essay on Singapore titled

"Disneyland with the Death Penalty".[31] Gibson's article left a lasting impact and has its own Wikipedia entry. A few commentators, including architectural theorist Rem Koolhaas and *New York Times* associate editor R.W. Apple, Jr., defended Singapore against Gibson's scathing critique. In 2020, Jerrine Tan, a Singaporean this time, also writing in *Wired*, revisited Singapore Gibson-style, looking out for more recent dystopian elements of "soullessness" like Changi Airport's Jewel.[32] But this time, this article did not go viral.

The world of global opinion has changed fundamentally. There is so much content now online that news and opinions about Singapore may make international headlines occasionally, but the sting of anything negative is just not the same as before. And even if any lasting impact is made, in any case, audiences for mainstream media keep on declining. At the same time, new channels and platforms emerge from everywhere. Sources of information have become so segmented and fragmented that just as it is now much more difficult to get everyone's attention, it is also, correspondingly, easier to recover from any scandal or reputational damage. Indeed, hardly anyone calls Singapore a "nanny state" anymore. To younger people both in and outside the country, this reference would probably even have to be explained.

A new Singapore:
The 2011 and 2015 general elections

There is always a new brand Singapore, that keeps on evolving all the time. Importantly, the very character of Singapore changed in the first half of the 2010s. The political nature of Singaporeans began to be revealed in very real ways during the 2011 and 2015 general elections. Also, the whole approach of government was transformed, resulting in a society that is more attractive in many ways to citizens and outsiders alike.

The 2011 election saw a 6.46 percentage-point swing in valid votes against the ruling People's Action Party from the 2006 election to 60.14 per cent, its lowest winning margin since independence. The PAP won 81 out of 87 seats, but for the first time, a Group Representation Constituency (a team of five seats), Aljunied, was lost to the opposition. A more vocal electorate was concerned about issues including politicians and government officials being out of touch with the ground and inadequate provision for healthcare and for the needy.

The political lessons learnt from this surprising result triggered a very substantial shift in the approach of the PAP, especially in increased social spending. As for public consultation, PAP Members of Parliament became much more active and visible on the ground, and also friendlier and more accessible online. Prime Minister Lee Hsien Loong is the most prominent example, with more than 1.5 million likes on his Facebook account in mid-2020. This has contributed directly to Singapore's 19th placing (second in Asia after Japan at number 7) in the 2016 *Soft Power 30 Report*, a ranking of the top 30 countries on soft power based on surveys of 10,500 people in 25 countries. This Report described Lee as "an incredibly skilled operator in the world of digital communications" who uses his Facebook "online proxy" internally to "help residents to feel more empowered in the political process and invested in the state" and externally as "a multi-purpose political tool that allows him to communicate domestic and foreign policy, support diplomatic efforts and advocate for Singapore around the world".[33]

For social spending, as then-Deputy Prime Minister Tharman Shanmugaratnam said in 2013, there has been a shift in government thinking since 2007 on social policy and helping the lower-income: "Now I would say the weight of thinking is left-of-centre. You still get diversity of views in Cabinet, but the centre of gravity is left-of-centre."[34] This shift led to new initiatives such as the slew of social benefits for the "Pioneer generation" of elderly Singaporeans, those who were aged at least 16 in 1965. There is no doubt that this major adjustment in social policy helped the PAP in the 2015 general election to score its best result since 2001 with 69.86 per cent of valid votes, an increase of 9.72 percentage points from the 2011 election.

The ruling party's resounding 2015 victory only reaffirms Singapore's key brand attribute of political stability. This has become even more of a valuable asset when contrasted with the political upheavals around the world, especially in Britain and the USA, but also elsewhere, such as in Chile and other parts of South America, sparked by discontentment over issues such as income inequality. At the same time, Singapore's "centre-left" shift in social policy has gone a long way towards bolstering the "good nanny" aspect of a government that looks after the basic needs of the people well. This was expressed very well by Prime Minister Lee Hsien Loong in an interview with *Financial Times* in 2014 when he was asked for his take on the status of Singapore as a "nanny state": "I think the fairways are wider. It doesn't mean there are no limits but it means there is more free play... When people say they don't want a nanny state, they are, in fact, in a conflicted state of mind. On the one hand, they want to do whatever they want and not be stopped. On the other hand, if something goes wrong, they want to be rescued."[35] Here, he is putting a positive spin on the nanny state by highlighting the good points of a nanny – she is, after all, the one who looks after the welfare of one's children and household.

Singapore has a unique capacity to preserve the "semi-permeable membrane" protecting it from negative outside influences. This it has demonstrated many times over – to make Singapore the best home for the good guys but also to make sure the bad guys keep away, to champion economic freedom but curtail media licence, to engender creativity but embed self-censorship. To achieve this juggling requires having, at the start, a high degree of control over one's circumstances – exactly the quality one would expect to find in the skills repertoire of any self-respecting nanny. As the world's knee-jerk aversion to nannies continues to recede, being able to have one's cake and eat it[36] might actually be Singapore's most unique and useful brand attribute, one that will do it much good for the long term, whether or not the nanny ever leaves the building. As an opinion piece on *BBC News* concluded in 2013: "The era of government-knows-best is slowly coming to an end in Singapore. No-one is quite sure what will take its place."[37]

The 2020 general election: A maturing democracy?

Politics never ceases to surprise, and openness to new revelations was to prove useful once again in the 2020 general election, which was expected to pave the way for a transition to the ruling party's fourth-generation (or "4G") leadership under Finance Minister Heng Swee Keat, who was promoted to Deputy Prime Minister in May 2019. With the polls held in July 2020 in the midst of the Covid-19 pandemic, some political observers predicted a "flight to safety" mentality among voters, akin to the circumstances around the general election of 2001, held soon after the 911 attacks in the US which sparked the "global war on terror". An opposition wipe-out was also seen to be on the cards, and some foresaw a

PAP winning margin as high as 75 per cent. Instead, the PAP took just 61.24 per cent of the valid votes, with the Workers' Party campaigning mainly on denying the ruling party a "blank cheque", to win 10 of the 93 seats, including a historic second Group Representation Constituency.

Initial analyses suggested that a new voter segment had emerged and needed to be accommodated – those who had a strong desire for more openness, transparency, accountability and social justice, as well as more effective efforts by the government to address issues including inequality, unfair treatment of minorities and climate change. Some saw a long-term trend of wanting more checks and balances in Parliament continuing from 2011, with 2015's high score for the PAP an aberration because of one-off factors including the emotive reminders of gratitude from the passing of founding Prime Minister Lee Kuan Yew.

In the aftermath of GE2020, once again, a new normal is finding a new equilibrium. One main impact of GE2020 on brand Singapore is to show foreign political observers that the political culture of what has been seen as "soft authoritarianism" and patronage is more complex than some had presumed previously. Socio-political harmony is one brand attribute that sets Singaporean elections apart from those abroad.[38] A default aversion to conflict is the basis for Singapore's envied political stability and predictability. This is a mindset built on key factors including one-party dominance over six decades from 1959, the ingrained gratitude of the older generations,

constraints on political discourse and civil society, and a sup-
portive mainstream media. Even if an opposition wipe-out
had materialised this time, an electorate conditioned to prize
solidarity would have accepted it with less rancour than in
many other countries.

The bread-and-butter worries of famously pragmatic
Singaporeans were also less influential on the voting trends
than predicted. Despite the retreat from globalisation across
the world, in Singapore, nativist, protectionist sentiments
typically hold weak appeal – below the global average level,
it would seem – because Singaporeans are well-adjusted to
job market competitiveness. This is an outcome of decades
of labour policies welcoming foreign talent and skills, and
the unique tripartite partnership of government, employers
and labour unions. Labour relations have been so harmonious that voting out the trade union chief is a non-issue, as
happened at Sengkang GRC, the second GRC to fall to the
opposition.

Political norms in Singapore have always prioritised
harmony, with sore losers criticised and opposition politicians
shunned for transgressions no more egregious than speaking
rudely to senior officials. Since independence, this tranquil
island has never harboured any real risk of street protests like
those against inequality in Chile or racism in the US. Today,
this political serenity is not being overturned by online public
opinion, but may, paradoxically, hinge on it. As long as there
is Wi-Fi, Singapore's netizens now know they wield the power

– on social media platforms and petition websites – to oust unsuitable candidates or rally to stand by those they wish to protect. One could say this is people power, Singapore-style. It is a positive side to what most Western commentators had often seen as nothing more than the denial of civil rights.

With the GE2020 result, a new political vision is winning support – a future in which socio-political harmony becomes even more inclusive, because power is shared with the people, and greater respect accorded including for alternative views, press freedom and artists. Going forward, the ruling party's first instincts will surely be to rebuild harmony as soon as possible; all the better to tackle the stern challenges of Covid-19 and its ensuing deep recession. At the same time, the political culture and consensus need to be refreshed. The PAP showed early signs of trying to adapt to understand voter segments such as younger digital natives who have a different view of what is acceptable online speech.[39] In a magnanimous move, Workers' Party chief Pritam Singh was officially named Leader of the Opposition, and given additional resources and parliamentary privileges.

These and other changes might herald a maturing of Singapore's democracy and a more balanced era in politics. Overall, recent political developments are clearly a plus for brand Singapore. As for the broader landscape as a whole, the challenges and opportunities of the future are surveyed in greater detail in the next chapter.

CHAPTER 7

REMAKING SINGAPORE – OVERCOMING COVID-19

New and future branding challenges assessed

SINGAPORE HAS BEEN remade and rebranded many times, and now, it must surmount the challenges brought by the disruptions of Covid-19. From 2015, a long-term initiative was already underway to rethink the super-long-term future of Singapore looking towards "SG100" – to the year 2065, 50 years ahead of 2015, the golden jubilee of independence. This effort is commendable for its far-sightedness, which is unsurprising for Singapore, given its brand attributes of political stability and social cohesion. To start the "SG100" visioning process, a public exhibition was held at Gardens by the Bay towards the close of the "SG50" year, called "The Future of Us". This multimedia exhibition sought to forecast and imagine the next five decades and what the future might hold for Singaporeans. The focus was primarily domestic, but one lasting effect, if only indirectly for some viewers, was on Singaporeans' sense of themselves and of their country and its place and character in the world.

Prior to this, the last major rebranding initiative led by the government was launched in 2010, called "The Spirit of Singapore". It was based on a realisation that Singapore's longstanding brand attributes of being "safe, reliable and efficient" were no longer enough for strategic brand differentiation in the global "war" for talent and investments. Indeed, Singapore's solid fundamentals are excellent examples of what are sometimes referred to by branding practitioners as merely "hygiene factors", things necessary but not sufficient for a country to get into the top league of nations – and to stay there. With the Covid-19 pandemic, the usual hygiene factors are being re-prioritised, and some are plummeting down the pecking order, as hygiene itself has become the paramount concern.

"The Spirit of Singapore" brand refresh was prompted by the realisation that brand Singapore needed something more. "We need also to have a message that reaches out, that touches the heart, moves the spirit and stirs emotions," said Lui Tuck Yew, then minister for information, communications and the arts, the man at that time overseeing the job of refreshing Singapore's nation branding. Speaking at a branding event in 2010, Mr Lui noted that government agencies had previously branded Singapore in various ways, with taglines such as "Uniquely Singapore", "YourSingapore", "City in a Garden" and "World of Opportunities". But while such individual campaigns have been successful to some degree, "none has shown how broad is the richness of what Singapore has to offer as a whole".

"The Spirit of Singapore"

The branding effort called "The Spirit of Singapore" is today no longer spoken of in specific concrete terms, the catchphrase all but forgotten. Its spirit and broad ideas have become embedded into the psyche and operational "DNA" of the Singapore civil service as it went back to business as usual – building up the ingredients that can boost economic growth, and not so much consciously and directly enhancing the country brand. Nonetheless, this branding exercise remains the most recent overt government-led initiative for country branding. It offers a case study of an effort by the public sector to see how Singapore could brand itself better by taking an enlightened approach, starting "upstream" in the branding process by focusing first on the underlying core brand values. This is applied by showcasing traits such as creativity, confidence and a "dare-to-dream attitude". Formulated by commissioned brand consultants as a new branding package mainly for internal use by public servants, there were four key brand attributes of Singapore as a country that were identified:

1. "Nurturing",
2. "Transforming",
3. "Collaborating" actively, and
4. Known for "daring to dream".

The intriguing aspect of this branding is that the term "Spirit of Singapore" is used internally to guide the branding efforts of all government agencies in what is called a "whole-of-government" (WOG) approach, but there is hardly any obvious external, explicit and visible manifestation and use of the term "Singapore Spirit". Neither is there any overall buzzword or tagline. Instead, the aim is for the newly articulated four elements of this nation rebranding to be surfaced organically in many different places and ways. The idea is to allow the people to fill in their own meaning and interpretation of what makes up, or makes for, the Singapore spirit. The conundrum, though, is how to achieve overall brand recognition – what Mr Lui calls "the richness of what Singapore has to offer *as a whole* [emphasis added]" – without a unifying umbrella messaging and positioning, but by aiming to express four brand attributes that not everyone may embrace? Would there be too many sub-messages? Do the messages themselves gel with the worldview and outlook of ordinary Singaporeans? To what extent is it necessary for ordinary citizens to be conscious of the key brand attributes?

This nation rebranding programme was seen by the government as being launched within a "brand lag" situation, in which the prevailing perceptions globally had not kept pace with the current reality of Singapore's at-times dizzying new vibrancy. This is because most foreigners who have never visited Singapore draw their impressions from what they read in the media, and increasingly, what they see online, or from hearsay, and some of these viewpoints are misinformed or out of date, while some are rehashes of older, prejudiced or inaccurate perspectives.

The main aim of this nation brand refresh was to counter what recent public surveys had shown since this rebranding effort first went to the drawing board in 2006. Locals and foreigners polled believed that Singapore had four major minuses: The place (1) has no "X factor", (2) is one-dimensional with a focus on the economy, (3) does not contribute to global issues, and (4) is not well-known to an international audience. These findings remain largely true, except for (1), as I would argue that Singapore's multiculturalism has come much more to the fore in recent years against a global backdrop of some quite ugly examples of racism and other forms of discrimination and marginalisation across many countries.

But this advance is tempered by point (4) about the need to boost and update awareness of brand Singapore among international audiences.

To address these negative perceptions, the government – through the inter-ministry National Marketing Action Committee at that time, an agency that no longer exists in this form – was mulling over implementing six new initiatives:

1. Creating narratives on the lifestyle, culture and entertainment in Singapore;
2. Getting Singaporeans to be ambassadors to market the country;
3. Having a panel advise the government on how to brand Singapore better;
4. Identifying an X factor;
5. Cultivating the foreign media; and
6. Raising Singapore's voice on global issues.

The desire to "create narratives on the lifestyle, culture and entertainment in Singapore" latched onto one of the keys to great nation branding – the quest for focused substance examined earlier in this book – and for this substance, the more authentic and distinctive it is, the better. Yet, the best way forward might be to avoid giving in to the temptation to overly direct this process, as in fronting the usual suspects or pre-selecting winning projects. Instead, a better approach would be to foster a more conducive environment for a natural flowering of talent, proof points and ideas from the ground up.

The global city era

The first 40 years of Singapore's independent history – from 1965 to 2005 – can be said to be Singapore's "manufacturing era", one led by an economic growth strategy whose centre of gravity was made up of the factories, research centres and supply chain networks set up by multinational companies mostly from the developed economies of the USA, western Europe and Japan. The phase of growth arguably emerging around the start of the millennium and gearing up from around 2004 can be called "the global city era". The concept of the "global city"[1] builds on the earlier work of academics such as Dutch sociologist Saskia Sassen of Columbia University and the London School of Economics. It is also informed by other theories of why people gravitate towards global cities, such as those surrounding the concept of a "creative class" by American urban studies theorist Richard Florida of the University of Toronto. Florida's theory suggests that the world's most creative cities thrive on attracting the best of three "T" factors: technology, talent and tolerance. Today, it looks as if 2019 – the last year of the pre-Covid-19 world – marked the height of this era that saw the great flowering of globalisation. What key aspect will define the post-Covid-19 world remains to be identified.

Singapore had stated its aim to be seen as Asia's "global city" – dynamic, distinctive, vibrant, sustainable.[2] The tagline for the 2006 International Monetary Fund/World Bank meetings in the republic was: "Singapore: Global City, World of Opportunities". A national strategy for Singapore to be "*the* global city in Asia" (emphasis added) was drawn up by the Economic Strategies Committee in 2009.[3] The aims include building Singapore up as a thought and practice leader in various areas, including place management – the art of making good places even better.

Significantly, the "global city" epithet for Singapore is one that more and more observers identify with,[4] and appreciate, as something that even comes with an added element of brand differentiation – becoming a global city "the Singapore way".[5] This alludes to an intriguing set of paradoxes about the country, such as how it is taking a centralised approach to facilitate many decentralised pockets of opening up, both in the hard world of industry, business and financing, as well as in the "soft" world of lifestyle and entrepreneurship in fostering the springing up of lively districts across the island living out the Singaporean civil service's catchphrase to "live, work and play" all in one place, exemplified by what former prime minister Goh Chok Tong once called "little bohemias".[6] As George Yeo famously said when he was the minister in charge of information and the arts: "We have to pursue this subject of fun very seriously if we want to stay competitive in the 21st century".[7]

Let the five stars sparkle freely

Singapore has many of the accumulated assets and achieved advantages to be a leading global city, although the global landscape has been altered significantly. Even before Covid-19 surfaced, serious questions were already being asked of the very idea of globalisation itself, as de-globalisation swept across the world and once-unheard of trade tariffs became a new norm in the ongoing tensions between the US and China. Most observers would concede that the golden age of globalisation is well and truly over. Global free trade, in theory, is a wonderful thing, maximising what the 19th-century British economist David Ricardo called "comparative advantage" to bring the greatest benefit to the greatest number of people around the world. But on one side of the globe, many people in places like rural and heartland America lost their jobs as factories moved to lower-wage locations overseas, while on the other side, factory smog threatens the health of many workers toiling in places like China, and persistently low wages hamper efforts to improve the livelihoods of millions everywhere. Still, until some concept other than globalisation takes over the imaginations of those who have the power to try to steer the global economy, Singapore's best bet at leading the rankings of country brands is by being an attractive global city, in spite of all the questions being asked by the pandemic.

One of the key brand attributes of a global city is live-ability, which has become so much more precious with the onset of Covid-19, and here, Singapore has been in a very good position for a long time. Since 1995, human-resource consulting firm Mercer – together with partner firms and quality-of-life experts – has been compiling a liveability index for cities. Cities in the survey are rated according to 39 factors, ranging from the ease of buying fresh fish for the kitchen table, to the reach of law enforcement. In its 2019 survey of 231 cities, Singapore came in 25th, the highest in the Asia-Pacific, especially on quality of life and personal safety, while Vienna, Austria, continued to top the global charts. Singapore has held the top spot in Asia since it over-took Tokyo in 2004.[8]

Another indicator of Singapore's standing as a global city is when other competing cities refer to it as competition. For instance, Sydney, which some observers rate as Australia's only global city,[9] sees Singapore, Hong Kong and Shanghai as its regional rivals. Singapore's standing in the global community of liveable cities has advanced significantly through the work of agencies such as the Centre for Liveable Cities. The Centre's work includes managing the World Cities Summit Mayors Forum, an annual gathering of more than 100 city mayors each time, to share best practices in making cities more liveable.[10] Aside from its other achievements, this forum adds value to Singapore's country brand through the perceptions of the mayors, public officials and other urban development practitioners who attend the event, which has been held in Singapore, Bilbao, New York, Suzhou and Medellín (Colombia).

Looking ahead beyond the worst of the Covid-19 disruptions, the future still looks bright for Singapore in nation branding, for what it can offer in the Asia-Pacific, especially given recent trends in the surrounding region. The world today could be at an inflection point in the development of global cities. Half the world's population is now urban for the first time in human history, after millennia of mostly agrarian existence; at the same time, half the world's most globalised cities are Asian. This will provide an excellent continental springboard for Singapore to continue to do well in its nation branding as Asia's pre-eminent global city.

In the 2019 A.T. Kearney Global Cities Outlook list, Singapore overtook San Francisco, New York and Paris to come in second among the world's most global cities. The Index uses definitive sources to tally everything from a city's business activity, human capital and information exchange to its cultural experience and political engagement. Data ranged from how many Fortune Global 500 company headquarters were in a city to the size of its capital markets and the flow of goods through its airports and ports, as well as factors such as the number of embassies, think-tanks, political organisations and museums. The global shift towards Asia, tracked for some years now, is clear: "There is no question which way the momentum is headed: Just as more people will continue to migrate from farms to cities, more global clout will move from West to East."[11]

Singapore continues to lend the benefit of its experience

to help other aspiring cities climb the ladder of global cities, for instance, assisting Mumbai to become a global city by 2052, advising on various aspects of urban planning and development.[12] Such projects will enhance Singapore's nation branding not only by profiling the country as a leader in this space but also its enlightened international relations, as seen in its willingness to share its knowledge, itself an attractive brand attribute.

A major nation brand-building challenge for Singapore, going forward, will be the extent of buy-in from the people themselves, and how they will relate to the proposed government initiative of having more Singaporeans acting as internal brand ambassadors. While fielding celebrities and recognisable public faces can do a lot for nation branding – as Hollywood actress Michelle Yeoh did for the "Malaysia, Truly Asia" campaign – ultimately a country brand soars or sinks with the level of everyday support from ordinary folk.

America is well-known for the high visibility of patriotism throughout the country, as seen in signs ranging from little American flags poked into ice-cream sundaes at Swensen's restaurants in California to the Stars and Stripes proudly emblazoned everywhere, whether it is a rodeo in Texas or a hot dog stand in Alaska. In Singapore, in the past, some Singaporeans would appear less than enthusiastic about participating in nation branding, but things have changed with the greater awareness of the country brand brought about by citizen engagement during the "SG50" year of 2015.

This was seen, for instance, in the almost annually revived talking point about the ubiquity, or lack thereof, of displays of the national flag around National Day. To some extent, this lower level of contribution to nation brand-building in this way had been reinforced by the official regulations allowing the flying of the flag only on flagpoles and illuminated at night, except for the three months around National Day from 1 July to 30 September, which is itself a relaxation only in 2007 allowing the flag to be displayed at all unofficially.[13]

In 2020, these flag regulations were loosened to allow people to fly the flag from April onwards, earlier than the usual start in July, so as to boost expressions of national solidarity during the "circuit breaker" partial lockdown to flatten the curve of Covid-19 infections. The fact remains that these regulations could be lifted completely. Freeing up the flag once and for all for patriotic expression can only have positive effects on nation branding, as well as adding to the brand personality of the flag itself, by, for example, giving it a name like "the Five Stars", as has been suggested in public feedback.[14] This idea is inspired by other countries whose flags have names, including Britain's Union Jack, America's Star-Spangled Banner, Japan's Nisshoki ("Sun-marked Flag") and Malaysia's Jalur Gemilang ("Stripes of Glory"). Such a move would add personality to the Singapore flag, to make it "come alive", and by extension, also help boost the brand personality of the nation itself.

Brand Singapore on the ground

Another key aspect of the future of brand Singapore is the character and personality of Singaporeans themselves. The "Ugly Singaporean" who displays anti-social behaviour used to be mentioned from time to time for actions such as jumping queue or not flushing public toilets. More recently, a greater sense of graciousness is emerging, through such government-led efforts as the Singapore Kindness Movement, as well as factors such as the "peer pressure" effect of social media. However, deeper negative facets of the Singaporean character will be harder to modify, if not eradicate. One of these is the flip side of the "nanny" that appears to have been transferred, to some degree, from the state to citizens. This is represented by the phenomenon of Singaporeans as an "environmentally pampered" people, in the words of Howard Shaw, executive director of the Singapore Environment Council. He said: "I don't know of one other country in Asean where you can just drink out of a tap. Or your garbage, for example. For 90 per cent of the population, it's thrown down the chute and it's handled… it's out of sight, out of mind. So we become a bit of a nanny state and we have a nanny mentality, that nanny will do everything for us. And nanny is, of course, the Government."[15]

This "leave it to nanny" mentality applies to other sectors of society as well, such as media censorship, where one policy focus has been on public education, to get more parents to shoulder the responsibility of looking after their own children's access to media with tools such as parental locks for cable TV and the Internet, instead of thinking they can rely on the government to keep undesirable media content at bay and enforce the rules against the dissemination of such materials to minors.[16] Here is where the "paradox of liberty" applies – only with more basic control can there be more freedom; only with more extensive participation in the protection of minors can adults themselves get more room for access and expression.[17]

The extent to which Singaporeans are willing to buy into anything like the "Spirit of Singapore" nation rebranding will go some way to sustain or subvert any internal country branding efforts. The trouble with the four key brand attributes proposed – transforming, daring-to-dream, nurturing and collaborating – is that they seem to be couched in, and culled from, the lingo and worldview of civil servants whose job is to market Singapore to high-priority, high-value foreign audiences, rather than aspects that gel and connect with the experience of the man in the street. For example, "daring to dream" has a long history as an organisational core value of agencies such as the Economic Development Board[18], so it is much better-known among civil servants than the man in the street.

There is also what has been observed as the typical ordinary person's disengagement from "grandiose" expressions of what National University of Singapore geography professor

Pow Choon Piew calls the "exhibitionary complex"[19] of Singapore's public sector agencies like the Urban Redevelopment Authority, for instance, in large-scale development projects around the redevelopment of places such as Marina Bay. It is left to the daily work of place branding to engage the average person by bringing such mega-projects down to a more relatable human scale. Or, take the observation of Singapore Management University sociologist Chung Wai Keung, who thought that the "Spirit of Singapore" nation branding is hard to back up. "Daring to dream is definitely not what the education system in Singapore teaches the students here," he says. If the branding effort is not matched by other related programmes, "it is almost like putting the cart before the horse".[20]

To some extent, the doubts expressed in 2010 about the "Spirit of Singapore" nation brand concept were valid, but they also were deviating from the main intent behind that brand refresh, in the sense that the four brand attributes are essentially for upstream application, meant to guide and inspire those who work on place branding – that is, people like the public servants who work in Singapore's economic agencies. The four terms are not meant for direct communication to the public without contextual articulation, application and elaboration. Such an upstream focus on conceptual brand attributes is the purist branding practitioner's approach. Some would even go so far as to avoid any kind of tagline or slogan – the domain of the downstream marketing practitioner – because this would mean narrowing and limiting the possibilities for brand expression. In this way, the "Spirit of Singapore" brand exercise is quite different from the "Passion Made Possible" of 2020, where the tagline is totally intended for the widest public communication and dissemination. Perhaps a blend of both approaches would be the best way forward for the future promotion of brand Singapore.

National metaphors and analogies – *sampan* or cruise ship?

In place branding, national metaphors can be a separate area of study all by themselves. These metaphors are distinct from analogies that might apply to a particular aspect of a country – for example, the lion as Singapore's national animal might be taken to represent characteristics such as strength and bravery, but it is not holistic enough to encompass the entire spirit and character of a nation. Some countries, like Switzerland, claim not to have any national metaphors. Japan has its *sakura*, the cherry blossom tree that can reflect both resilience in overcoming adversity such as severe winters to make its eventual blossoming all the more precious, as well as the fragile beauty that is at the heart of its *wabi-sabi* aesthetic that celebrates the seemingly imperfect wonders of nature. New Zealand is an intriguing example, where some people consider the national metaphor to be the "number 8 wire", originally the preferred wire gauge for sheep fencing in remote farms, which is firm yet flexible, that came to be a metaphor for the ingenuity and resourcefulness of New Zealanders. Bhutan has no official national metaphor, but if it wanted one, it need look no further than its *druk* (dragon) symbol from ancient history, that is totally in sync with the grandeur and grace of the mountain kingdom's heritage of monarchy.

In the case of Singapore, there is no one universally agreed national metaphor, but one traditional candidate makes for an interesting case in terms of influencing the citizens' capacity to dream big on the world stage, which is a crucial internal aspect of a country's everyday brand ambassadors. For many years, Singapore was often described as a *sampan*, the Malay word for a very small wooden boat, typically used for fishing or for ferrying passengers in shallow waters. This had previously been a favoured image, especially among politicians, for Singapore's small land size and vulnerability, and the consequent need to avoid "rocking the boat". Over the years, Singapore had also been compared to other seacraft including a ferry boat, "a sturdy boat with a good rudder and a strong sail", in a speech by former trade and industry minister George Yeo.[21]

However, the signs are there for an upgrade on the kind of seafaring vessel that Singaporeans should imagine themselves to be sailing on. In October 2013, in an opinion column in *The Straits Times*,[22] I argued that Singapore, given all its internal and external developments and achievements over the years, and taking into account its global assets such as its substantial sovereign wealth fund, had grown beyond being compared to a *sampan*. Instead, the column argued that the republic was now more like a small cruise ship, which is in fact more sophisticated, and – contrary to the easy perception that a cruise is just a holiday – it is even harder to upkeep than a *sampan*. The next day, however, Prime Minister Lee Hsien Loong told the Singapore media at a press briefing in Paris, France, that he disagreed with the suggested new national metaphor. He maintained that Singapore was still a *sampan*, albeit an upgraded version, which he called "Sampan 2.0",[23] sparking some discussion online in Singapore and abroad.

However, a few months later, Mr Lee appeared to have changed his stance, apparently having reconsidered the inadequacy of the *sampan*. Speaking on a TV programme on *Channel NewsAsia* in September 2014, he said: "We are a small country. We used to say we are a *sampan*, now maybe we are a boat with a motor, self-propelled."[24] A year later, during the hustings for the general election of September 2015, Emeritus Senior Minister Goh Chok Tong described Singapore, led by the ruling People's Action Party through five decades, as "a cruise ship with a definite destination".[25] This Singapore "ship", he added, had been well-steered by three prime ministers including himself, unlike the risky "casino ships" and "cruises to nowhere" offered by the opposition.

For the longest time, typical conversations in Singapore in which someone expressed a desire or ambition to do something would attract, before long, a comment from someone else that Singapore is just a small country, and so, the market is too tiny, the talent pool too limited, or some other such deflating idea. But in fact, if one looks back in history, there is a case to be made that, even by the early- to mid-19th century, Singapore had already grown beyond its *"sampan"* conditions when Raffles landed to become likened more as a "Chinese junk", the seacraft that brought thousands of migrant workers, merchants and others, braving the expanse of the South China Sea to seek their fortunes on this little island. More recently, a shift in global outlook to view Singapore as a stronger vessel than in previous decades has been prompted by events including the winning of an Olympic gold medal for Singapore by swimmer Joseph Schooling at the Olympic Games in Rio de Janeiro, Brazil, in 2016. For one thing, it is no longer possible to suggest that Singapore is too small a country to produce an Olympic champion. Developments like Schooling's win can go quite some way towards dispelling any lingering old small-town mindset. This is where any continued insistence on invoking the *sampan* for obviously political purposes would be totally at odds with the simultaneous goal of inspiring Singaporeans to "dare to dream" of excellence in other areas of life.

It had seemed then as if the *sampan* had – finally – been sunk, and so, this could have marked the beginning of a new phase of country brand awareness among ordinary Singaporeans that would stand brand Singapore in good stead for the future. However, maritime imagery was to bob up to the surface again, at the general election of July 2020. A newly founded party, Red Dot United, campaigned on the belief that Singapore should be seen as "a confident ocean liner", on which Singaporeans could navigate the challenges of today as "captains of our own lives".[26] Its party manifesto cited PM Lee's 2013 metaphor, arguing that a "sampan 2.0" would be vulnerable and weak, and swing about precariously in the tides of the times.

As a metaphor, the "ocean liner" has the advantage of avoiding the misguided knee-jerk reaction to a "cruise ship" of immediately visualising people lazing about on deck-chairs. Also, the comparatively sparser interior furnishings on board an ocean liner would make it a more suitable metaphor for the Covid-19 era, when many of the luxuries and "finer things in life" have been put on hold. But, demonstrating the impossibility of any one metaphor satisfying all requirements, the ocean liner also leaves out the element of high-roller tourism in a global city that had come to have the Marina Bay Sands Hotel and Casino as one of its most-recognised landmarks internationally – this is a facet of the new Singapore that the cruise ship more adequately captures.

During the GE2020 hustings, Mr Goh – who retired from politics just before the election and was commenting on his own Facebook page – again warned voters not to rock the Singapore *sampan,* despite calling Singapore a cruise ship in the previous general election of 2015. "I had to steer our tiny Singapore *sampan* through many choppy waters – economic recessions, financial crises, terrorist threats and SARS (Severe Acute Respiratory Syndrome)," he wrote. "We did so safely because Singaporeans rowed together with me. I will never forget the unity and support from fellow Singaporeans in times of crisis."[27] He also commented that Singapore's political scheme of having Non-Constituency Members of Parliament was devised in the early 1980s by him and Mr Lee Kuan Yew, so as to "secure the *sampan* with outriggers", because the stability of "sampan-sized" Singapore was always at the back of their minds. With political checks and balances guaranteed by always having NCMPs as opposition voices in Parliament, he added, "you can put a sail on the *sampan*, catch the wind and go fast without fear of it capsizing. The NCMP scheme is an important outrigger for our political system."[28]

A tiny *sampan* seems so out of sync with how well-stocked Singapore is in reality, as well as with what is then expected of it, given its resources. This was borne out by how GE2020 also introduced one other important aspect of the socio-political maritime imagery for Singapore – the plight of marginalised minorities, especially at a time when the international spotlight was being increasingly placed on issues of inequality. One sample public comment on Mr Goh's Facebook page was that, after 50 years of development, the team in government should be able to "upgrade" Singapore to a "big ship" like a *bahtera* (ark) so as to venture further out to sea than would be possible with a *sampan* made for coastal waters. Similarly, Workers' Party candidate Raeesah

Khan likened the poorest members of society to "those who had already fallen from the boat and are drowning",[29] and a bigger, better boat should be one that welcomes everyone as equal stakeholders, all able to live with dignity. Sentiments like these add to the calls for an upgrade on the vessel of Singapore as it charts a new course through to the post-Covid-19 world.

So, is Singapore a flimsy boat or a sturdier ship? One way to reconcile the inherent contradictions might be in the difference between analogy and metaphor – while a small seacraft like a *sampan* could serve as an analogy to highlight a single, specific attribute of tiny size and weakness, after more than six decades of Singapore's development, a bigger, better-equipped vessel like a cruise ship or ocean liner would be more suitable as a national metaphor for the whole country. After all, while the revival of the *sampan* in GE2020 invokes the old political narrative of vulnerability, a vessel that can afford more than S$100 billion (around US$73 billion) of pandemic relief measures looks more like a cruise ship or ocean liner.

And so, the *sampan* might not have sunk completely, since old mindsets apparently can still launch it for the occasional foray, usually for political purposes, but when this happens, the *sampan* should be seen only as an analogy for the aspect of vulnerability. But surely, after GE2020, enough passengers have made it clear that a bigger, better vessel, like a cruise ship or ocean liner, is preferred as a national metaphor to give confidence to everyone on board that the captain and crew are in full command of the resources required, and available, for the journeys ahead.

Is Singapore "future-ready"?

One piece of nation branding wisdom is that, for global brand perceptions about a country image to really change, the reality has to change first. For example, if South Africa had not abolished apartheid, no amount of advertising would have made the soccer World Cup Finals that it hosted in 2010 the success that it was in enhancing brand South Africa. Then the "*waka waka*" in the theme song by the singer Shakira would have remained just a song and dance and no more. Simon Anholt, guru of nation branding, thinks that South Africa should build on what it has achieved not by looking forward and seeking to mirror developed nations but by looking back at lessons from the continent's history and heritage and exercising leadership to help other African nations improve their lot. This, in turn, would further enhance its own nation branding.[30] What governments actually do, instead of only what they say, is the key to a successful nation branding effort.

This approach of "do as you say" is what Singapore has always tried to adhere to, in its typically pragmatic way. For example, the Economic Development Board launched the brand concept "Future-Ready Singapore" to a world audience of potential investors in the 2010s as the next big thing for the city-state.[31] The key idea is that Singapore is always "future-ready", a place that is well-equipped to welcome and embrace the future in all its aspects, from maximising new growth opportunities and nurturing creativity, innovation and R&D, to test-bedding new technologies and processes, while always looking ahead and imagining future scenarios. This branding was first rolled out to international audiences at the World Cities Summit 2010 in Singapore, and is also being promoted by other Singaporean economic agencies, with "future-ready" added to the civil service's lexicon of key buzzwords. This concept would be an ideal platform to express the key brand attributes of the umbrella nation rebranding under the "Singapore Spirit" concept.

Once again, this kind of nation branding is targeted mainly at overseas audiences, but its ultimate success could hinge on whether it can get ordinary Singaporeans to also buy into it, to help fulfil its full potential. This is where this brand aspect connects with the Smart Nation plan, where the state has to work towards smart governance, as PM Lee has said: "You want to create possibilities so that your successors will have choices. That means you need very competent people, and a lot of information – 'big data' – and you must be able to pull it all together to make sense of the data and to respond to it, in real time or strategically over the long term."[32] However, a key success factor will be in one of the chief aims of a smart nation – to mobilise the citizens and the community to embrace a new level of digital connectedness.

Digital connectivity empowers people to aspire towards global achievement for themselves and their communities, at the same time contributing to the country brand.

Brand concepts such as "Future-Ready Singapore" speak mainly to multinational companies, big-time investors and top foreign talent. For the man in the street, the future is also about large-scale events that have a dimension of engaging the general public. In a *Business Times* feature in August 2010, business heads were asked what they thought could be the "next big thing" for Singapore to look into for global brand-building, after the two integrated resorts, the Formula One night race and the inaugural Youth Olympic Games.[33] There were some good ideas in there. Kowshik Sriman, the managing director of software company SAP, advocated "organic growth", that is, focusing more resources on Singaporean shows, events and attractions that have the potential to become global brands, including organisations that serve educational and conservation purposes, such as the Science Centre Singapore, Singapore Zoological Gardens, Singapore Botanic Gardens and National Museum of Singapore, to help them learn from and emulate world-renowned ones like the Smithsonian Institution in Washington, D.C., USA, and the Guggenheim Museum in Bilbao, Spain. Another idea, from Dora Hoan, group CEO of Best World International Ltd, was for Singapore to host an event like the World Expo, held in Shanghai in 2010 and in Milan in 2015. This global event runs for six months, is known to attract over 70 million visitors, and has been the birthplace of icons such as the Eiffel Tower, first presented at the 1889 World Expo. Yet another idea, from Tan Kok Leong, principal of TKL Consulting, was for Singapore to be the Asia headquarters of world bodies that promote international diplomacy and other causes, to mitigate and minimise international conflicts.

What these suggestions show is that there are many more things that can be done to enhance Singapore's nation branding. In the global nation branding game, there is no such thing as "job done", only an unending effort of branding, brand management and rebranding. In Singapore's case, the city state – politically conditioned over the years to keep running an endless marathon of self-improvement – has already achieved a remarkable amount in what has often been called its ability to "punch above its weight". Even this tired cliché from boxing is in need of a refresh, reeking, as it does, of a hard power mentality, when an image from the lexicon of soft power would be so much more enticing. The country does have a very solid foundation, with many friends and admirers around the world across the entire spectrum of nations, developed and developing. To stay in the nation branding game and keep moving up the charts, Singapore certainly has some challenges in its way. But there is never any shortage of capacity for strategic thinking and political will, just as there are tremendous resources at its disposal to call upon in investment and implementation. The political leadership and public sector have done much. Perhaps what remains is to take up the adaptive challenge[34] to unleash the full potential of its people and private sectors. And then, the small but robust and resilient national imagery of Singapore can really become something else.

The overall initial impact of Covid-19

How did the onset and initial phases of the Covid-19 pandemic affect brand Singapore and Singapore's efforts in country branding? In February 2020, Singapore was hailed in a Harvard University study as a "gold standard" among nations in managing the coronavirus outbreak.[35] Four epidemiologists at Harvard's T. H. Chan School of Public Health wrote: "We estimated that detection of exported cases from Wuhan worldwide is 38 per cent as sensitive as it has been in Singapore." But by April, a significant outbreak in Singapore's foreign workers dormitories had surfaced, and, with aggressive testing, more than 56,000 cases had been found by end-August. This led some commentators to switch to referring to Singapore as a "cautionary tale" instead.

And so, Singapore slipped from the "gold standard" status, but the republic's inherently effective capabilities in public health and pandemic response, which had been internationally recognised earlier, came to be praised once again, later on. The original physical segregation of migrant workers' accommodation turned out to be what enabled the ring-fencing of the virus from the wider community, and so, helped contain the outbreak. To apply a very rough analogy – one that is quite Singaporean – this is a bit like Singapore as a top student who later doesn't do so well in one subject. Migrant worker management is a very important subject, to be sure, but still, it is one subject in a larger "curriculum" of pandemic challenges that is still testing – and examining – every nation. The commendations in the international media later in the year for the republic's overall crisis response included an op-ed in the British newspaper *The Independent* in August 2020 describing Singapore as "the safest part of the world, where they knew what to do and acted with great speed to aggressively suppress the lethal virus".[36]

Singapore stood out in its well-resourced and concerted response from the earlier situation, and this was a brand recovery as much as a physical recovery. To cater to the welfare of the migrant workers, there was a comprehensive commitment of dedicated resources for isolation, treatment and rehabilitation, more than most other countries could, or would, have mustered. The help for these workers, who had to be quarantined and tested systematically, was drawn from more than S$100 billion of relief measures, which were funded, unlike in most other countries, from national reserves and largely without borrowing.

The republic's already well-known excellence in healthcare was affirmed by key statistics such as having one of the lowest deaths of any country – only 27 by the end of August, which works out to a rate of less than 4 per million, compared with a three-digit number in most countries, such as 632 per million in Britain. Singapore also saw very few serious cases – only 128, or 0.3 per cent of cases, in intensive care by August 2020, compared with ICU beds being maxed out across some countries such as the USA.

However, amidst all this, there were a couple of missed opportunities. Singapore could have won more friends around the world if it had offered expressions of international solidarity similar to how Switzerland projected digital images of the flags of other countries on the face of the Matterhorn during the early months of the pandemic. The Singapore flag was projected onto the mountain peak via live webcam in April,[37] but Singapore did not reciprocate this gesture. Another example was if more effort had been made to enhance the visibility of aid efforts to China and other countries. This is not to blow one's own trumpet, but to help narrow the perception gap – an area of longstanding brand deficit – that Singapore typically does not do enough in the international arena to assist other nations who need help.

How Covid-19 affects the four main sub-brands

The impact on brand Singapore's four main sub-brands of trade, investment, tourism and immigration has also been positive, overall. For trade, up to a third of global trade has passed through Singapore, along the Straits of Malacca, since the 13th century, when the island was called Temasek. Traders supplying say, ice-cream from Australia to Japan have always known that it is faster and cheaper not to ship directly but to go through Singapore and rely on its efficiency and frequency of transshipment. Singapore's value as a transshipment hub explains how it has remained the world's second-largest port by cargo volume since the 1970s when it was second to Rotterdam, and has remained number two today (after Shanghai) even when Rotterdam dropped to the world's 11th, because the Dutch port is a gateway port more dependent on Europe's economic vibrancy in its surrounding region, as opposed to a global transshipment hub like Singapore.

With its inherent and longstanding advantages as a trading hub, Singapore's port reputation in the aftermath of Covid-19 has the capacity to become even stronger. It has already adjusted and diversified its sources and partners to set up an even more reliable and distributed supply chain network that now can include shrimp from Saudi Arabia or hen's eggs from Poland, so as to help global traders not to literally put all the eggs in one basket. But while its sea hub is still bustling, Singapore's air hub has suffered much more, with air traffic down to a tiny fraction of its pre-Covid-19 level of 20 million passenger movements a year through Changi Airport.

As Singapore works to rebuild its air hub, the country's brand attributes of determination, dynamism and enterprise, as well as the optimism and self-confidence engendered, are captured in a botanical metaphor used by Transport Minister

Ong Ye Kung. On a visit to Changi Airport's Terminal Two (which was closed temporarily to save costs), he saw that the indoor decorative bougainvillea there had withered, but learnt that these hardy plants would grow again – "underneath the dried brown bark was a bright green stem". Making Changi Airport full again, and Singapore Airlines planes soar once more, is "our collective mission in the coming months and years ahead, as we await the blooming of the bougainvillea once again".[38]

For investment, Singapore still has the fundamentals to ensure a strong pipeline of projects to grow the economy. In May 2020, the EDB announced S$13 billion in investment commitments for the January–April period of 2020, which was already higher than the full-year projection of S$8–10 billion.[39] Singapore remains a "safe harbour" for investors like Uber, which delayed the shift of its Asia-Pacific headquarters to Hong Kong until at least the end of 2022, partly due to Covid-19-related and political developments in the Special Administrative Region. And this harbour, clearly, is still a place of promise for the future – in September 2020, Apple opened its first "store on the water" in a spherical pavilion on the waters of Marina Bay, on Singapore's most iconic down-town promenade. By the same token, the city-state is a haven for individual investors such as Eduardo Saverin, James Dyson and Jet Li (now a Singaporean), who, by their personal exam-ples, in turn, act as brand ambassadors for Singapore. Like them, other high-net-worth individuals are also looking for places that have brand attributes that meet the concerns over stability, safety and taxes, while offering attractions including material aspects such as all the creature comforts and intangible qualities such as a cosmopolitan society.

As for inventory control, Covid-19 has spurred a major shift in global business practice from the previous "just in time" efficiency model to cut storage costs to a "just in case" model for a more robust system, to cater for unpredictable emergencies like pandemics. Whether for the main or backup supply, it would make sense to deal with a place as *kiasu* (afraid to lose) as Singapore, where there will be some wastage in being prepared, but there is a better chance to catch any new opportunity. Also, Singapore will remain important as a hub for Southeast Asia and the world, as it has always been. Now, this role will see another phase of revival, with the rise of what has been called the "China plus one" strategy to have, in addition to China, a second location as a base for regional management, R&D and logistics.

For tourism, any recovery will first go to those places that are perceived as safe, trusted and welcoming – all longstanding brand attributes of Singapore. The Singapore Tourism Board is poised for eventual recovery, with a comprehensive plan of action. Meanwhile, it is working on initiatives such as the "SG Clean" programme to certify places of business as being well-equipped and practised in Covid-19 safety measures. With inbound tourism practically decimated, a $45 million programme, SingapoRediscovers, was launched in July by STB, Enterprise Singapore and Sentosa Development Corporation to promote domestic tourism[40] – this initiative contains potential for some internal brand-building to enhance the sense of place among Singaporeans, in addition to all the dollars-and-cents considerations. Both internally and externally, the rich reservoir of brand equity earned from more than three years of promoting the "Passion Made Possible" brand concept will stand Singapore in good stead.

For immigration and relocation to Singapore, those looking to study at all levels might find Singapore more appealing now that educational institutions overseas, such as Ivy League universities in the US, have almost all moved to online classes. As for those seeking to work and live in Singapore, the above aspects are pluses. On top of that, there is the X factor of multiculturalism in a country where the signature of social harmony and mobility could not be clearer, when there is a Muslim head of state, an Indian leader of the opposition in Parliament, and a Eurasian Olympic gold medallist.

Brand Singapore's value for future growth

The future of the economic aspects of brand Singapore in a post-Covid-19 world could hinge on three key factors. First, as more economic activity moves online, Singapore will need to hasten a successful migration into the post-pandemic digital economy. Here, it can count on its earlier investments in shaping up to be a smart nation, including new technology such as 5G networks. The EDB's "global entrepolis" concept – of Singapore as a place uniquely positioned to catalyse innovation and investment with its entrepot, enterprise and entrepreneurship elements – becomes even more viable as more economic activity moves online, and hence, to connect with anyone and anywhere else in the world.

Second, in a world made even more unstable by Covid-19, Singapore will need to be adept in navigating through the rougher terrain of US-China geopolitics. What it has in its favour are all the advantages that accrue to its many decades of enlightened relations with the big powers. This is the foundation that explains why US companies are the biggest investors in Singapore, with more than 20 per cent of all Foreign Direct Investment, exceeding all Asian companies combined, while China is Singapore's largest trading partner and the number one destination for outbound FDI.

Third, Singapore will need to become even more active in its participation in multilateral frameworks such as modified versions of the Trans-Pacific Partnership, which was earlier derailed by the world's shift towards deglobalisation in the second half of the 2010s. Singapore, as one of the main longstanding torchbearers of free trade, will surely stay at the forefront of any pathways of multilateralism through a global trading system ravaged by the pandemic. In this arena of multilateralism and rules-based systems in the global order, Singapore has earned for itself over many decades a solid reputation for trustworthiness. This strong brand attribute of Singapore is the backdrop, for example, to a Singaporean being elected as the first Asian director-general of the Geneva-based World Intellectual Property Organisation – Daren Tang, who was chief executive of the Intellectual Property Office of Singapore. Wipo is responsible for shaping global rules for intellectual property and oversees trademarks, designs and patents.[41]

Coming to the internal dimension of the impact of Covid-19 on brand Singapore, two facets have seen significant increase – moderation and charity. The government, corporate sector and people in general have had to contend with a recalibration of what had been deemed as symbols of success previously, some of which included elements of excessive materialism. Conspicuous consumerism such as lavish nightlife activities came to a halt. These adjustments could even come to strengthen Singapore's brand essence.

Also, Singaporeans showed that they have heart – charity giving to the three main national donation platforms in the first five months of 2020 reached S$90 million, already equalling the whole of 2019. Volunteerism sprouted everywhere, from sewing masks to food delivery to the needy. The worst of times brought out some of the best in humanity – the brightest spot in these troubling times. Overall, then, the times are certainly tough but there are many reasons for optimism about the future of brand Singapore through Covid-19, and long after.

Singapore's orientation to the world

In summary, once the worst of the Covid-19 pandemic is over, can Singapore move up to the next level of the nation branding game? Where will it stand? How will it do on its strengths and weaknesses? There is no doubt that Singapore is unusually good at positioning itself to the rest of the world, and overall it seems as if it does a better job of nation branding externally than internally – that is, it channels more attention and resources to influencing the world's opinions and perceptions than those of its own citizens. This priority remains the case, even though the relative weightage has shifted after the "SG50" year of 2015, with a citizenry roused to become more assertive in civic participation. The balance will surely shift further, after the key lessons in voter expectations of more intangible aspects from the general election of 2020 are responded to.

To illustrate Singapore's clear focus on external audiences, take the heritage initiative by the National Heritage Board since 2010. The unveiling of a sculpture of Chinese leader Deng Xiaoping along the Singapore River[42] was timed with the visit to Singapore in that year by China's then vice-president, Xi Jinping. This public artwork is part of a series of heritage markers commemorating visits to Singapore by public figures revered in other countries. The previous three luminaries so honoured were the novelist Joseph Conrad of Poland, national hero Jose Rizal of Philippines and revolutionary leader Ho Chi Minh of Vietnam. The effect of this heritage initiative is to deepen Singapore's foreign relations more than it is to engage its own people. It is something that very few countries do, or would even think of doing. Most nations are too busy honouring their own citizens who are major heritage figures or, at most, global figures who are substantially more meaningful to those countries, for example, home museums remembering writers such as Franz Kafka in Prague, in the Czech Republic, or the memorial to Portuguese explorer Vasco da Gama at the Cape of Good Hope in South Africa. Singapore, however, is sometimes accused – as it was with the public feedback on this series of markers to prominent visitors – of paying more attention to the foreign than to the indigenous. This is a charge not without some merit.

This typical Singaporean orientation towards international recognition and approbation is also a pervasive motivation in many other spheres of life. The whole effort of economic development since the early 1960s has focused more, on balance, on attracting foreign enterprise than on growing homegrown companies and entrepreneurs. Homegrown small and medium enterprises have long complained about the relative lack of priority for them. It is not that there is no help at all for the local, there are many schemes, but it is the degree of the difference that is striking. This imbalance has been redressed somewhat but the tilt in favour of the foreign persists.

In general, there is seldom prolonged hesitation to put money behind programmes geared towards investing in foreigners. One such example is the $10-million Community Integration Fund to co-finance activities that will help foreigners and new immigrants "bond" with citizens.[43] A greater willingness to apportion substantial public money drawn from Singapore's massive coffers to what are essentially programmes that will add to nation branding would place Singapore further ahead of other nations in the branding game. Needless to say, those nations that lack the finances, political will and concerted focus on wooing the outside world will never catch up. The key question that remains is whether Singapore can really challenge its leading competitors, when those rivals include brand giants and even bigger spenders such as China, whose nation branding intentions and resources are ambitious and very clear, for instance, in showpieces at home such as hosting the Olympic Games in Beijing in 2008, and the World Expo in Shanghai and Asian Games in Guangzhou in 2010 on the trot, followed by external initiatives such as the Belt and Road initiative to revive the ancient overland and maritime Silk Roads across the whole Asian region and connecting to Europe and beyond.

Multiculturalism's X factor and Singapore's standing

The big question is whether Singapore can continue to score big on its nation branding on the economic front, despite some minus points in the socio-political realm. The initial evidence appears to suggest that it is possible to do this. As earlier observed in this book, the two spheres can be compartmentalised quite well, and the key factor in this is the extent to which the citizenry and corporate players are willing – more than willing, in most cases – either to accept the needed compromises for personal gain or to ignore the issues altogether. The possibility for this ideological ambivalence and co-existence is perhaps summed up by the fact that in 2010, for instance, the controversies over contempt of court (the case against British writer Alan Shadrake for his book on Singapore's death penalty, *Once A Jolly Hangman*) and the lack of the kind of civil liberties that most Westerners are used to (cited, for instance, during the debate over the proposed merger deal between the Singapore and Australia stock exchanges) resurfaced in a year of record economic growth.

Judging from most nation branding surveys, Singapore was holding its own and improving its standing before the pandemic. Today, on Singapore's strengths and weaknesses in summary, its country brand is as robust as ever and growing stronger on the hardware angle, in aspects such as infrastructure, public safety, education, jobs, skilled workforce, attractiveness for investment and environment for raising children. Some of these aspects – such as jobs and investments – will come under further strain in the aftermath of the Covid-19 pandemic. Singapore will have to put on its economic and urban planner's thinking caps and work to remake its economy once again. One issue, especially with the workplace disruptions brought about by the pandemic, will be how to strengthen what has been called the "Singaporean core" of the workforce, while maintaining that increasingly rare brand attribute of openness to immigrant talent. This was a key item on the agenda of the new term of Singapore's 14th Parliament, sworn in in August 2020. As for the "softer" lifestyle aspects, Singapore had been consolidating its position and moving up the ranks on such international rankings not only on facets like nightlife, food and shopping, but also other areas like heritage and culture. The brand equity already earned on these and other factors is a firm foundation for market recovery when the worst of Covid-19 eventually passes.

The world after Brexit in the UK and under a USA led by President Donald Trump was already presenting new challenges that suggest that the old methods of country brand differentiation may no longer work in the same ways. Country borders were becoming less open and welcoming than before, even as internal ethnic, religious and other divisions have eaten into societies everywhere. Hence, people who are deciding where next to trade, travel to, or relocate to study, work or seek a better life have had to recalibrate their assessments. Covid-19 has totally complicated everything. Internally, larger countries can get things going first with revived domestic economic activity including tourism. But globally, only those nations with strong brands will see immediate signs of recovery.

Here, one of Singapore's unique selling propositions – its best country branding X factor[44] – could be its unusually high level of social cohesion and harmony. Social stability is at a level and quality of resilience that some other countries would wish for. This is so despite the fact that Singapore society is welcoming many new members all the time, on a daily basis. Even if Covid-19 has slowed down this process, the long-term trend should resume as soon as travel restrictions are relaxed. Only around three out of five people on the island are citizens, about 3.5 million among the 5.7 million population in 2020. About one in three new marriages are between a Singaporean and a foreigner. The 22,500 new citizenships granted in 2018 was the highest figure in 11 years.[45]

As more immigrants are integrated, the resulting cultural shifts taking place can be discerned in, for example, how the Hindu festival of lights, traditionally known by its Tamil name *Deepavali*, is becoming just as often referred to by its Hindi name *Diwali*, reflecting the different cultures of more recent immigrants from the Indian subcontinent, compared with those from earlier decades. Meanwhile, *Chap Goh Meh* (the 15th day of the Lunar New Year, usually known by its name in Hokkien, the largest dialect group among the Chinese in Singapore) is just about holding its own against its Mandarin name, *Yuan Xiao*.

Singapore's social cohesiveness can be captured in another national metaphor – that of a "flower dome of multiculturalism", which could be the "X factor" that respondents had suggested, in surveys conducted for the "Spirit of Singapore" branding exercise in 2010. The essence of this multiculturalism is alluded to in the lines below from my poem titled *Flower Dome Singapore*, published in *The Straits Times* in 2016:[46]

> *in a universe where DNA can just vanish without trace,*
> *this is one way for identity, community, to seed, to be retained:*
> *optimal conditions, conditioning, always trading space*
> *for serenity, often offering up openness to be constrained*
>
> *for livelihood is embraced as a harvest of mastering the elements,*
> *adjusting to co-exist, accepting fruit from promises of sustenance*

Gardens by the Bay, a futuristic public garden that is one of Singapore's top tourist attractions, has two biodomes. One of them is called the Flower Dome, where plants from cooler climates have been imported and transplanted. Here, they thrive well, with help from a carefully tended new habitat, adjusting temperatures and keeping disease and pests at bay. In the same way, Singapore as a country is, in some ways, just as well-managed – for example, through social policies such as the ethnic quota scheme in public housing estates – to nurture the most conducive "total environment" to attract talent, tourism, trade and investments from all over the world.

How Singapore can keep nurturing the conditions for its way of life, and keep moving up the rankings and strengthening its international reputation, remains to be seen. The quality of its initiatives to boost its country brand will, in all likelihood, have an even more crucial role in a post-Covid-19 world of even fiercer rivalry for attention and approval, brand awareness and brand affinity. To achieve more of such success will require more investment, focus on needed areas of improvement and coordinated response, in the crucial, complex process – and unavoidable game – called nation branding.

ENDNOTES

Notes to Introduction

1. See, for example, questions from students from mostly small states in "The place of country branding in public policy: a case study of Singapore", talk by Koh Buck Song, moderated by Aaron Maniam, on the YouTube channel of Blavatnik School of Government, Oxford University, 30 Jan 2018.
2. "Person of the Year", *Time* magazine, Dec 2016.

Notes to Chapter 1

1. See *The Smartest Guys in the Room: The Amazing Rise and Scandalous Fall of Enron*, Bethany McLean and Peter Elkind, Portfolio Trade, USA, 2003.
2. See, for example, "Myanmar's new capital: Remote, lavish and off limits", *The New York Times*, 23 Jun 2008.
3. "South Africa asked to join emerging powers bloc", CNN, 24 Dec 2010.
4. "Donald Trump has destroyed the country he promised to make great again", Fintan O'Toole, *The Irish Times*, 25 Apr 2020.
5. The concept of comparative advantage is credited to the English political economist David Ricardo (1772–1823), who explained it in his 1817 book *On the Principles of Political Economy and Taxation*.
6. George Yeo, Minister for Foreign Affairs, at a Foreign Correspondents' Association talk in Singapore, 24 Jun 2005.
7. For example, the 2006 controversy over cartoon depictions of the Islamic Prophet Muhammad in a newspaper in Denmark has since led to many more images, from online spoofs to real-life graffiti, featuring turbans as a motif.

8. "Canada now has the world's most Sikh cabinet", Ishaan Tharoor, *The Washington Post*, 6 Nov 2015.

9. See, for instance, an essay on the history of the term "winning hearts and minds" in "A bright shining slogan", Elizabeth Dickinson, *Foreign Policy* magazine, Sep/Oct 2009.

10. For example, the USA was ranked top in the Country Brand Index 2009 (produced by the consultancy FutureBrand and BBC World News, and covering 102 countries) but dropped to fourth in 2010.

11. "The Merlion gets a makeover by Salvatore Ferragamo", Charlene Fang, *CNNGo*, 10 Nov 2010.

12. These include the Eiffel Tower of Paris (built for the 1889 World's Fair, the precursor to today's World Expo), and the Little Mermaid of Copenhagen (based on the 1837 fairytale by Danish writer Hans Christian Andersen).

13. See, for example, "Is this the greatest PR stunt ever?", *BBC News Magazine*, 7 May 2009.

14. See, for example, "Australia attacks on Indians 'opportunist' crimes, envoy says", Bibhudatta Pradhan and Paul Tighe, *Bloomberg Businessweek*, 6 Jan 2010.

15. See, for example, "The national flag of Singapore", *Singapore Infopedia*, National Library Board, at www.nlb.gov.sg.

16. See the *MyStory* website of Singapore's National Heritage Board at www.nhb.gov.sg.

Notes to Chapter 2

1. *Heart Work: Stories of How EDB Steered the Singapore Economy from 1961 into the 21st Century*, lead author Chan Chin Bock, edited by Koh Buck Song, Singapore Economic Development Board, 2002.

2. See the World Economic Forum's 2019 ranking at www.weforum.org.

3. See, for example, *Singapore: The Unexpected Nation*, Edwin Lee, Institute of Southeast Asian Studies, Singapore, 2008.

4. At the National Day Rally speech in 2002, then-Prime Minister Goh Chok Tong said: "Singapore needs a few little Bohemias where artists can gather to soak in the ambience, and do their creative stuff."

5. Interview with Lee Kuan Yew, then Senior Minister, "In wooing investors, even trees matter", Koh Buck Song, *The Straits Times*, 1 Aug 1996.

6. See the Corrupt Practices Investigation Bureau's media release at https://www.cpib.gov.sg/press-room/press-releases/singapore-maintains-high-score-transparency-international-corruption, accessed Aug 2020.

7. "Corruption is perceived as almost non-existent", says the Heritage Foundation of Singapore in its 2010 Index of Economic Freedom.

8. See, for example, *How Not to Make Money: Inside Stories from Singapore's Commercial Affairs Department*, Koh Buck Song, CAD, 2002.

9. See, for example, the essay "The English Language in Singapore: Lens and Launchpad to the World" by Koh Buck Song in *200 Years of Singapore and the United Kingdom,* edited by Tommy Koh and Scott Wightman, Straits Times Press, Singapore, 2019.

10. See, for example, *Celebrating 50 Years of Excellence as the Regional Language Centre of Choice*, edited by Koh Buck Song, Jasminder Kaur and Elsa Yow, Regional Language Centre, Singapore, 2018.

11. "Pisa tests: Singapore top in global education rankings", Sean Coughlan, *BBC*, 6 Dec 2016.

12. For more details, see the website of the Infocomm & Media Development Authority of Singapore at www.imda.gov.sg.

13. For more information, see the Singapore Tourism Board website at www.stb.gov.sg.

14. Tan Chin Nam, then chief executive of the Singapore Tourist

Promotion Board, quoted in "Singapore set for challenges of 21st century tourism", *The Jakarta Post*, 4 Oct 1996.

15. "Worldwide net contest to promote Singapore", *The Straits Times*, 20 Apr 1996.

16. A dedicated website for the YourSingapore branding is at www.yoursingapore.com.

17. This broad-based reputation was the reason for Singapore's jump in rankings such as the FutureBrand Country Brand Index, in which the republic moved from 24th place in 2008 to 11th in 2009, reported in "Asia's national brands rise in profile", Kenny Lim, *Media*, 19 Nov 2009.

18. Singapore Tourism Board website 24 Aug 2017.

19. For more details, see the *Impossible Stories* website of the Economic Development Board at www.edb.gov.sg/en/impossible-stories.

20. See, for example, one of the few pieces of international media coverage for this event: "Singapore embarks on cultural diplomacy with France", *Xinhua News Agency*, 14 Sep 2010.

21. "Spotlight on Singapore in South Africa", Tay Suan Chiang, *The Straits Times*, 9 Oct 2010.

22. For more information, see the Singapore Media Fusion website at www.smf.sg.

23. "Growing Singapore's presence on the global media stage", *Business World* advertorial, 9 Aug 2010.

24. "In Singapore, a new cultural vision", Joyce Lau, *The New York Times*, 8 Dec 2015.

25. "Singapore film festival aims to be Asia's Cannes", *Reuters*, 4 Jun 2010.

26. "Restoring forests: The green manifesto", *India Today*, 20 Sep 2010.

27. "A changing role for public service", speech by Ngiam Tong Dow delivered at the Ministry of National Development's Speaker Series, published in *The Straits Times*, 8 Sep 2006.

28. See the Gardens by the Bay website for more info at www.gardensbythebay.org.sg.

29. "Taking back the waterfront", George Wehrfritz and Sonia Kolesnikov-Jessop; with B. J. Lee in Seoul and Jonathan Adams in Taipei, *Newsweek International*, 16 Jan 2006.

30. "An emerald isle – Singapore's plans to get even greener", Cris Prystay, *The Wall Street Journal Asia*, 31 Oct 2008.

31. "How urbanised Singapore is learning to live with its wildlife", Chew Hui Min, *Channel NewsAsia*, 22 Aug 2020.

32. For more details, see the "City in Nature" website of the National Parks Board at www.nparks.gov.sg

33. For more information, see the Night Safari website at www.wrs.com.sg.

34. Speech by Prime Minister Lee Hsien Loong, 2010 Singapore Energy Lecture, Singapore International Energy Week, 1 Nov 2010.

35. See, for example, *Engineers as Urban Systems Innovators: How Innovative Engineers Helped Build a Liveable and Sustainable City*, edited by Koh Buck Song, Centre for Liveable Cities, Singapore, 2019.

36. "Singapore Has a S$100 Billion Plan to Survive in a Far Hotter World Than Experts Predicted", Faris Mokhtar, *Bloomberg*, 26 Feb 2020.

37. For more information on the Asia-Pacific Economic Cooperation (Apec) forum, see www.apec.org.

38. "The 'Asian Switzerland': Why Singapore has been chosen to host Trump-Kim summit", Chris Graham, *The Telegraph*, 10 May 2018.

39. "Singapore, 'Switzerland of the East'", *The New York Times*, 21 Jan 1973.

40. Prime Minister Lee Hsien Loong, speaking at the official opening of Fusionopolis, 17 Oct 2008.

41. "Advisory council's vision for Singapore – a Global Entrepolis", Denesh Divyanathan, *The Straits Times*, 1 Mar 2003.
42. "Transformed Singapore's new attractions prove strong draw for Middle East visitors", *Middle East North Africa Financial Network*, 29 Jul 2010.
43. "Disneyland with the death penalty", William Gibson, *Wired* magazine, Sep/Oct 1993.
44. "Singapore race is tops with many fans", Sanjay Nair, *The Straits Times*, 27 Sep 2010.
45. "Formula One: Ecclestone sees 20-year future for Singapore GP", *Agence France-Presse*, 26 Sep 2010.
46. See, for example, "Familiarity and uniqueness: Branding Singapore as a revitalized destination", paper by Dr Can-Seng Ooi, Copenhagen Business School, Denmark, Apr 2010.
47. Lee Kuan Yew's memoirs are published in *The Singapore Story* (1998) and *From Third World To First: The Singapore Story: 1965–2000* (2000), Marshall Cavendish, Singapore.
48. See the chapter "Romancing the American MNCs" in *Heart Work: Stories of How EDB Steered the Singapore Economy from 1961 into the 21st Century*, lead author Chan Chin Bock, edited by Koh Buck Song, Singapore Economic Development Board, Singapore, 2002.
49. Lee Kuan Yew, Global Brand Forum, 16 Aug 2004.
50. "'PAP has lost its way': Estranged brother of Singapore's PM Lee Hsien Loong backs new opposition party", *Agence-France Presse*, 28 Jul 2019.
51. "Govt prepared to pay political price over changes to Elected Presidency: Chan Chun Sing", Lianne Chia, *Channel NewsAsia*, 8 Sep 2017.
52. Comment on Facebook by Malaysian MP from the Islamic party Amana, Dr Siti Mariah Mahmud, Sep 2017.
53. "The Global Religious Landscape", Pew Research Center, USA, 4 Apr 2014.

54. Speech by PM Lee Hsien Loong, swearing-in ceremony for President Halimah Yacob, 14 Sep 2017.
55. "Brand Singapore gets unique boost", Koh Buck Song, *The Business Times*, 9 Nov 2017.
56. For a fuller discussion on the national self-confidence of former colonies, see, for example, "Will the British make Great Britain great again?", Koh Buck Song, *The Business Times,* 8 Feb 2020.
57. "The bicentennial's impact on brand Singapore", Koh Buck Song, *The Business Times,* 16 Nov 2019.
58. *Seven Hundred Years: A History Of Singapore*, Kwa Chong Guan, Derek Heng, Peter Borschberg & Tan Tai Yong, Marshall Cavendish, Singapore, 2019.
59. See, for example, "Three Things That Make Nation Branding Difficult", *Nation Branding*, at nation-branding. info/2010/04/03/3-things-that-make-nation-branding-difficult, accessed Sep 2010.
60. *An Inquiry into the Nature and Causes of the Wealth of Nations*, Adam Smith, W. Strahan and T. Cadell, London, 1776.

Notes to Chapter 3

1. See, for example, "Whither Singapore Inc.?", *The Economist*, 28 Nov 2002.
2. See, for example, Lee Hsien Loong's statement: "We will develop and invest in our people, but we also need to reinforce the Singapore team with talent and numbers from abroad", National Day Message, 8 Aug 2010.
3. See, for example, "Local SMEs can 'hunt in packs' abroad", Francis Chan, *The Straits Times*, 1 Apr 2010, in which Lim Hwee Hua, as second minister for finance, responds to the recurrent concern of weak Singaporean enterprises by urging the republic's companies to emulate their counterparts in Japan or Korea that have much more of a culture of "hunting in a pack".

4. See, for instance, "Branding excellence – the most important driver of value for Asian companies" at the branding website *All About Branding*, www.allaboutbranding.com/index.lasso?article=342, accessed Oct 2010.

5. *Only The Paranoid Survive: How to Exploit the Crisis Points that Challenge Any Company*, Andrew S. Grove, Broadway Books, USA, 2010.

6. See, for example, "The Singapore Girl", Michael Richardson, *The New York Times*, 8 Jun 1993.

7. "New wax figure of Singapore Girl launched at Madame Tussauds", Jocelyn Lee, *The New Paper*, 5 Mar 2015.

8. See, for example, the panel discussion "Who Are You? (Singapore Girl)" featuring Simon Obendorf, John Klang and Koh Buck Song, at the Substation's *Singapore Girl, or Heritage Deployed* programme, 6 Oct 2018.

9. "Raffles Holdings – The Lex Column", *Financial Times*, 19 Jul 2005.

10. For more details about the Singapore International Foundation, see the SIF website at www.sif.org.sg.

11. For more information on Asia Pacific Breweries, see the APB website at www.apbsingapore.com.sg.

12. "ChevronTexaco deal won't hit Singapore ops", Ronnie Lim, *Business Times*, 6 Apr 2005.

13. "Following change in CEO, Kulicke & Soffa to move HQ", philly.com, 10 Aug 2010.

14. "Dyson to move global HQ to historic Singapore building", *BBC*, 29 Nov 2019.

15. For a fuller account, see *Heart Work: Stories of How EDB Steered the Singapore Economy from 1961 into the 21st Century*, lead author Chan Chin Bock, edited by Koh Buck Song, Singapore Economic Development Board, Singapore, 2002.

16. "Film students roam world", Joanne Lee-Young, *Vancouver Sun*, 19 Oct 2009.

17. A recommendation from a Pacific Economic Cooperation Council sustainability tourism seminar in Tahiti, in "Tourism needs more 'cultural immersion'", Koh Buck Song, *The Business Times*, 1 Dec 2017.

Notes to Chapter 4

1. Tony Rayns' review is on the British Film Institute's Oct 2010 London Film Festival website at www.bfi.org.uk/lff/node/1089.
2. "Kirsten Tan's 'Pop Aye' is Singapore's Best Foreign Language Film pick for Oscars 2018", Boon Chan, *The Straits Times*, 25 Sep 2017.
3. *From Boys to Men: A Literary Anthology of National Service in Singapore*, edited by Koh Buck Song and Umej Bhatia, Landmark Books, Singapore, 2002.
4. "SG50 has stirred new Singapore spirit: Heng Swee Keat", *The Straits Times*, 28 Dec 2015.
5. See, for example, *Reproduction in Education, Society and Culture*, Pierre Bourdieu, with Jean-Claude Passeron, Sage, UK, 1990.
6. *Bound To Lead: The Changing Nature of American Power*, Joseph S. Nye, Jr., New York: Basic Books, USA,1990.
7. "The trick that Singapore missed", Koh Buck Song, *Today*, 20 Aug 2003, cited in *Soft Power: The Means to Success in World Politics*, Joseph S. Nye, Jr, Public Affairs, USA, 2005.
8. *Spiaking Singlish: A Companion to How Singaporeans Communicate*, Gwee Li Sui, Marshall Cavendish, Singapore, 2017.
9. "Why 'Mee Pok Man' should not be called 'The Noodle Seller'", Koh Buck Song, *The Straits Times*, 24 Jul 1995.
10. "We Cannes do it!", Genevieve Loh, *Today*, 5 May 2010.
11. "The Art of Sen", Mak Mun San, *The Straits Times*, 7 May 2007.
12. "Singapore goes to Paris", Adeline Chia, *The Straits Times*, 23 Sep 2010.

13. See, for example, "'Who's afraid of Catherine Lim?'", Seth Mydans, *International Herald Tribune*, 19 Sep 2009.

14. "Raintree Pictures 'The Leap Years' is main feature film at explorASIAN Festival", *Channel NewsAsia*, 13 May 2010.

15. *"Writing Singapore": An Historical Anthology of Singapore Literature*, edited by Angelia Poon, Philip Holden and Shirley Geok-lin Lim, NUS Press, Singapore, 2009.

16. "Charlie Chan: An Imaginary Cartoonist Draws A Very Real Homeland", Etelka Lehoczky, *National Public Radio*, 5 Mar 2016.

17. "The Real Economic History Behind 'Crazy Rich Asians'", Suyin Haynes, *Time*, 14 Aug 2018.

18. "Crazy Rich Identities", Kwame Anthony Appiah, *The Atlantic,* 25 Aug 2018.

19. "Crazy Rich Asians: Scoring big-time for brand Singapore", Koh Buck Song, *The Business Times*, 28 Aug 2018.

20. "Four who made their mark", *The Straits Times*, 22 May 2010.

21. "An Emergency in Art", Sonia Kolesnikov-Jessop, *Newsweek International*, 8 Oct 2007.

22. "A rare Dolphin in Singapore", Leong Weng Kam, *The Straits Times*, 14 Mar 2000.

23. "They flew here from LA just to see his art", Josephine Chew, *The New Paper*, 12 Nov 2004.

24. See the National Gallery Singapore website at www.nationalgallery.sg.

25. *The Bali Field Trip*, Kwok Kian Chow, at www.postcolonialweb.org/singapore/arts/painters/channel/12.html.

26. *The Adventures of the Mad Chinaman*, Dick Lee, Times Editions, Singapore, 2004.

27. See, for example, "Singapore and the 'Asian Values' Debate", Donald K. Emmerson, *Journal of Democracy*, Vol. 6, No. 4, Oct 1995, pp. 95-105, The Johns Hopkins University Press, USA.

28. Tommy Koh's contributions are documented in, for example, the book *Asia and Europe: Essays and Speeches by Tommy Koh*,

edited by Yeo Lay Hwee and Asad-ul Iqbal Latif, Asia-Europe Foundation and World Scientific Press, Singapore, 2000.

29. *The Little Red Dot: Reflections by Singapore's Diplomats*, edited by Tommy Koh and Chang Li Lin, World Scientific, Singapore, 2005.

30. See, for example, Kishore Mahbubani's book, *The New Asian Hemisphere: The Irresistible Shift of Global Power to the East*, Public Affairs, New York, USA, 2008.

31. See Prof Michael Porter's presentation at the launch of the Asia Competitiveness Institute in 2006 at the Harvard Business School website at www.hbs.edu.

32. "Kofi Annan to take up Li Ka Shing professorship next year", *The Straits Times*, 5 Sep 2009.

33. "Singapore hands over $3 million educational college to Sri Lanka", Relief Web website at www.reliefweb.int.

34. "The great cultural dessert", Macaw, Singapore, Mar/Apr 1994, quoted in *Theatre and the Politics of Culture in Contemporary Singapore*, William Peterson, Wesleyan University Press, USA, 2001.

35. Details of the Renaissance City Plan III and other arts strategy plans are available online at the National Arts Council website at www.nac.gov.sg.

Notes to Chapter 5

1. The inaugural Youth Olympic Games was held in Singapore from 14 to 26 August 2010, featuring athletes aged 14 to 18 representing 205 national Olympic committees.

2. *Malay Annals*, originally printed for Longman, Hurst, Rees, Orme and Brown, 1821, with an introduction by Sir Thomas Stamford Raffles; translated from the Malay language by John Leyden, National Library Board Singapore digital edition, 2008.

3. See, for example, www.sg, an information website on Singapore by the Ministry of Communications and Information.

4. Zoologist John Harrison, father of former Singapore Zoo curator Bernard Harrison, made this speculation in the 1960s, quoted in *The Straits Times*, 9 Aug 2001.

5. In 2001, the courtesy drive was subsumed into the Singapore Kindness Movement, a broader national initiative to enhance the living space on a crowded island. But Singa lives on, for example in an outdoor advertisement by the Singapore Kindness Movement in 2010 depicting Singa the courtesy lion on what looks like a cinema poster concept extolling the virtues of extending kindness to one's fellow citizens.

6. Cited in a speech by then Senior Minister Lee Kuan Yew at the inauguration of the relocated Merlion Park at the Singapore River, 15 Sep 2002.

7. Extract from the poem "Merlion: Strike One" by Koh Buck Song, in *Reflecting on the Merlion: An Anthology of Poems*, edited by Edwin Thumboo and Yeow Kai Chai, National Arts Council, Singapore, 2010.

8. "Kallang Roar born from a trip to Wembley", Jeffrey Low, *The Straits Times*, 3 Oct 2010.

9. "Merlion demolition plan upsets some but experts say Sentosa overhaul vital", Tiffany Fumiko Tay, *The Straits Times*, 22 Sep 2019.

Notes to Chapter 6

1. "The nanny state places a bet", Wayne Arnold, *The New York Times*, 23 May 2006.

2. "Why Singapore banned chewing gum", Elle Metz, *BBC News Magazine*, 28 Mar 2015.

3. "Hair? That's his antenna", Tan Kee Yun, *The New Paper*, 13 Feb 2010.

4. "Government's hard-nosed approach defended", *The Straits Times*, 20 April 1987.
5. "Who's afraid of Catherine Lim?", Seth Mydans, *The New York Times*, 19 Sep 2009.
6. For an assessment of Bhutan's country brand-building options, see "Can Bhutan take its happiness brand to the next level?", Koh Buck Song, *The Business Times*, 20 Apr 2019.
7. Tony Rayns' review is on the British Film Institute's Oct 2010 London Film Festival website at www.bfi.org.uk/lff/node/1089.
8. "Singapore woos singles in latest dating campaign", *Agence France-Presse*, 14 Aug 2010.
9. "Behaviour modification takes on many forms as Singapore shapes its citizens", Yeoh En-Lai, *Associated Press*, 8 Dec 2004.
10. The Economist Intelligence Unit's country risk briefing on Singapore, 12 Aug 2010.
11. "City confidential – Singapore: Functioning foodie heaven, or control-freak central?", Nina Caplan, *Time Out*, 30 Apr 2009.
12. "Sky high and splendid", Kevin Brown, *Financial Times*, 3 Jul 2010.
13. "A Sudden Coronavirus Surge Brought Out Singapore's Dark Side", Megan Stack, *The New York Times*, 20 May 2020.
14. "Nanny state? Singapore has its own buzz", Gabriel Chen, *The Straits Times*, 24 May 2007.
15. "More jail time for Swiss man in Singapore graffiti case", *The Globe and Mail* (Canada), 18 Aug 2010.
16. "Can a nanny state really rock?", Rahul Jacob, *Financial Times*, 4 Nov 2006.
17. "Can a nanny state really rock?", Rahul Jacob, *Financial Times*, 4 Nov 2006.
18. "The just-in-case committee of Singapore", *The Jakarta Post*, 19 Apr 2007.
19. See, for example, "Will the UK really turn into 'Singapore-on-Thames' after Brexit?", Howard Davies, *The Guardian*, 17 Dec 2019.

20. "Beijing to limit new car quotas in 2011", *Reuters*, 23 Dec 2010.

21. "What Singapore Can Teach the White House", William McGurn, *The Wall Street Journal*, 21 Oct 2009.

22. "Economics professor gives Singapore something to chew over", *South China Morning Post*, 31 Mar 2000.

23. "Gum returns to Singapore after 12-year ban", Gillian Wong, *Associated Press*, 26 May 2004.

24. "*Cosmopolitan* doing roaring sales in Singapore after 22-year ban lifted", *Agence France-Presse*, 7 Nov 2004.

25. See, for example, "Singapore eases gay ban", *BBC News*, 4 Jul 2003, citing remarks in an interview by then-Prime Minister Goh Chok Tong with *Time* magazine.

26. This was part of the government's stated response to the recommendations of the Censorship Review Committee 2010, available at the Ministry of Communications and Information website at www.mci.gov.sg.

27. "Singapore swing", David Lamb, *Smithsonian* magazine, 1 Sep 2007.

28. "Remade in Singapore", Kevin Hamlin, *Institutional Investor,* 12 Sep 2006.

29. "Apron strings to loosen on Singapore's nanny state – future PM", Karl Malakunas, *Agence France-Presse*, 7 Jan 2004.

30. "The nanny state places a bet", Wayne Arnold, *The New York Times*, 23 May 2006.

31. "Disneyland with the Death Penalty", William Gibson, *Wired*, 4 Jan 1993.

32. "The Fantasy and the Cyberpunk Futurism of Singapore", Jerrine Tan, *Wired*, 29 Jul 2020.

33. *The Soft Power 30 Report 2016.*

34. "Cabinet: More left-of-centre now, helping the lower income", Aaron Low, *The Straits Times*, 9 Apr 2013.

35. See, for example, "No surprise that Singapore's unique", Koh Buck Song, *The Straits Times*, 27 Apr 2005, on "how adept

Singapore can be in achieving its national goals while restraining perceived threats to the average citizen".

36. "Lunch with the FT: Lee Hsien Loong", *Financial Times*, 11 Apr 2014.

37. "Singapore's mid-life crisis as citizens find their voice", Jonathan Head, *BBC News*, 21 Oct 2013.

38. "Updated sociopolitical harmony could reshape a new era", Koh Buck Song, *The Business Times*, 15 Jul 2020.

39. "Younger Singaporeans to decide where to draw boundaries on discussions on race and religion: Shanmugam", Grace Ho, *The Straits Times*, 25 Jul 2020.

Notes to Chapter 7

1. See, for example, *The Global City: New York, London, Tokyo*, Saskia Sassen, Princeton University Press, USA, 2001, and *The Rise of the Creative Class*, Richard Florida, Turtleback, USA, 2003.

2. See, for example, remarks by Singapore's then-deputy prime minister, Teo Chee Hean, in "Singapore 'can stay forever young'", Zakir Hussain, *The Straits Times*, 6 Apr 2010.

3. For the report of the Economic Strategies Committee's Sub-committee on Making Singapore a Leading Global City, see the Ministry of Finance website at www.mof.gov.sg.

4. See, for example, "Singapore Swing: Playing for Wealth Crown", *Reuters*, 30 Sep 2010.

5. See, for example, "Relaxing Its Grip to Play for a Winning Hand", Norimitsu Onishi, *The New York Times*, 7 Jun 2010.

6. "Singapore can become an entrepreneurial society", Eugene Low, *The Business Times*, 19 Aug 2002.

7. The quote from George Yeo is included on an educational website called The Institute for Habits of Mind at www.institute-forhabitsofmind.com.

8. "Singapore tops quality of living ranking and personal safety for Asia: Mercer poll", Vivienne Tay, *The Business Times*, 13 Mar 2019.

9. See, for example, "Time for our city to shape up to global expectations", Stephen Loosley, *Daily Telegraph*, 3 Mar 2010.

10. See, for example, *Making Cities Liveable: Insights from 10 Years of Lectures at the Centre for Liveable Cities*, edited by Koh Buck Song, Centre for Liveable Cities, Singapore, 2018.

11. "Metropolis Now: The Global Cities Index", *Foreign Policy*, 1 Sep 2010.

12. "State plans global city by 2052", *Hindustan Times*, 4 Aug 2010.

13. For guidelines on displaying the national flag, see the National Heritage Board website at www.nhb.gov.sg.

14. Letter by a reader, Adrian Chan Pengee, writing to the Singapore newspaper *My Paper*, 1 Sep 2010.

15. "'We're environmentally pampered'", Venessa Lee, *TODAY*, 5 Jun 2010.

16. See the Censorship Review Committee 2009-10 Report at www.mci.gov.sg.

17. "The paradox of liberty", Koh Buck Song, *The Straits Times*, 9 Dec 1991.

18. See *Strategic Pragmatism: The Culture of Singapore's Economic Development Board*, Edgar H. Schein, MIT Press, USA, 1996.

19. See the essay "Critical Reflections on the Remaking of Singapore as a Global City" by Assistant Professor Pow Choon Piew of the Department of Geography, National University of Singapore, in the book, *Management of Success: Singapore Revisited, edited by Terence Chong*, Institute of Southeast Asian Studies, Singapore, 2010.

20. "Jumping on the brandwagon", Tan Hui Yee, *The Straits Times*, 10 Jul 2010.

21. Speech by George Yeo, Minister for Trade and Industry, Trade Development Board International Day, 9 Jan 2001.

22. "Sink the old *sampan*, S'pore now a cruise ship", Koh Buck Song, *The Straits Times*, 30 Oct 2013.

23. "Singapore remains a 'sampan', but an upgraded one: Hsien Loong", Sumiko Tan, *The Straits Times*, reprinted in international media including *The Jakarta Post*, 31 Oct 2013.

24. Lee Hsien Loong, *Channel NewsAsia*, 4 Sep 2014.

25. "GE2015: WP like a gambling ship that goes nowhere, says ESM Goh Chok Tong", Rachel Au-yong, *The Straits Times*, 6 Sep 2015.

26. "GE2020: In Jurong GRC, PAP commits to fairer, more inclusive society; RDU pushes for good jobs, more choices for people", Chew Hui Min, *Channel NewsAsia*, 5 Jul 2020.

27. "Singapore GE2020: Don't rock the 'Singapore sampan', ESM Goh cautions", Joyce Lim, *The Straits Times*, 8 Jul 2020.

28. "Singapore GE2020: NCMP scheme a 'stabiliser' for electoral system and a 'winning hand' for Singapore democracy, says ESM Goh Chok Tong", Joyce Lim, *The Straits Times*, 4 Jul 2020.

29. Raeesah Khan interview, Workers' Party candidate videos on Facebook for GE2020 at https://www.facebook.com/watch/?v=1129265820780085

30. Remarks by Simon Anholt to the Brand Africa 2010 Forum in Johannesburg, 16 Sep 2010, reported on the website bizcommunity.com.

31. See, for example, "Branding Singapore", *The Straits Times,* 28 Jun 2010.

32. For one of the earliest articulations of Singapore's smart nation vision, see "Lee Hsien Loong: Fulfilling the human spirit", interview by Koh Buck Song and Khoo Teng Chye, *Urban Solutions Issue 5,* Centre for Liveable Cities, Singapore, Jun 2014.

33. "The next big thing", Views From The Top, *The Business Times*, 23 Aug 2010.

34. The term "adaptive challenge" is used according to the definition by Ronald Heifetz of the Kennedy School of Government, Harvard University, in *Leadership on the Line: Staying Alive*

Through the Dangers of Leading, Ronald Heifetz and Marty Linsky, Harvard Business Press, USA, 2002.

35. "S'pore is gold standard for case detection: Harvard study", Rei Kurohi, *The Straits Times,* 18 Feb 2020.
36. "Singapore's quick response to coronavirus saved thousands of lives. There's no excuse for the UK's failure", Melissa Jacobs, *The Independent,* 4 Aug 2020.
37. "Singapore flag projected on Switzerland's Matterhorn in show of solidarity during coronavirus", *The Straits Times,* 24 Apr 2020.
38. "Truths to Keep Singapore Moving", National Day Observance speech by Transport Minister Ong Ye Kung, 14 Aug 2020.
39. "Singapore secured S$13b in investment commitments in Jan-Apr 2020; exceeds EDB projection", Janice Heng, *The Business Times,* 30 May 2020.
40. "Staycation deals, heartland tours part of $45m domestic tourism campaign to save local businesses", Tiffany Fumiko Tay, *The Straits Times,* 22 Jul 2020.
41. "IPOS chief Daren Tang becomes first Singaporean to helm global intellectual property agency", Grace Ho, *The Straits Times,* 8 May 2020.
42. "Sculpture to honour Deng", Ng Kailing, *The Straits Times,* 18 Nov 2010.
43. "96 ideas for integration", Vanessa Jalleh, *The Straits Times,* 18 Oct 2010.
44. "Protecting the X-factor in Brand Singapore", Koh Buck Song, *The Business Times,* 15 Jun 2017.
45. For data on Singapore, see the Singapore Department of Statistics website at www.singstat.gov.sg.
46. "Flower dome Singapore", Koh Buck Song, Rhyme & Reason literary series, *The Straits Times,* 4 Jun 2016.

INDEX

ABOUT THE AUTHOR

KOH BUCK SONG (family name: Koh) has been closely involved in the nation branding of Singapore for three decades, in various capacities. Most recently, he was a member of the Singapore Tourism Board's Marketing Advisory Panel for the "Passion Made Possible" brand concept launched in 2017.

As socio-political commentator, editor and journalist with *The Straits Times* (1988–99), he articulated and critiqued the Singapore brand for global and domestic audiences.

In strategic public communications since 1999, he has advised the Singapore government on nation branding, quality of life, economic strategy, foreign investment promotion, entrepreneurship, urban planning, leadership culture, national security, environmental stewardship, international media relations, market competition and policies on media, heritage, arts and culture. He served on many citizen panels such as the Singapore Arts Festival steering committee and as Deputy Chairman of the Censorship Review Committee 2010, after also serving on the committees of 1992 and 2003.

As head of global media relations and strategic planning for the Economic Development Board – a lead agency spearheading brand Singapore since 1961 – he led a team to create the "global entrepolis" brand concept for Singapore.

As head of public affairs (Southeast Asia) at communications consultancy Hill & Knowlton, his public-sector accounts included the global branding of Gardens by the Bay, Fusionopolis, National Gallery Singapore and the Singapore Garden Festival.

Koh has also advised foreign governments on country brand-building, soft power and bilateral relations, and has spoken on Singapore's global image at international conferences at Harvard University, Massachusetts Institute of Technology and Chicago University in the USA; as well as at Oxford University's Blavatnik School of Government; Fudan University in Shanghai; and Melbourne and Deakin Universities in Melbourne. He was the keynote speaker at the City Nation Place Global Forum in London, and has also spoken at the Japan Foundation in Tokyo on a visit as a cultural leader of Singapore; at a dialogue on nation building and branding at the Royal Institute for Governance & Strategic Studies in Phuentsholing, Bhutan; and at a Pacific Economic Cooperation Council seminar on sustainable tourism in Tahiti, French Polynesia.

As Adjunct Editor at the Centre for Liveable Cities of Singapore's Ministry of National Development, he authored numerous reports, including for the World Cities Summit Mayors Forum and the Young Leaders Symposium in Singapore and New York, as well as edited books including *A Chance of a Lifetime: Lee Kuan Yew and the Physical Transformation of Singapore* (2016). He has also been an editorial consultant for organisations including the FutureChina Global Forum, Urban Redevelopment Authority, National Environment Agency, Lien Foundation and Wildlife Reserves Singapore.

Koh holds a master's degree in public administration from Harvard University's Kennedy School of Government, where he was a Mason Fellow, as well as degrees in English from Cambridge University and in education from London University. He has lectured on leadership as Adjunct Associate Professor at the Lee Kuan Yew School of Public Policy, National University of Singapore; and on media policy at the School of Social Sciences, Singapore Management University.

This is his 36th book as author and editor. The first edition of *Brand Singapore* was translated into Chinese and published in China in 2012. His other books include *Heart Work* (2002) and *Heart Work 2* (2011), on Singapore's global branding for foreign investment promotion; *Perpetual Spring: Singapore's Gardens By The Bay* (2012), the official coffee table book of Singapore's futuristic public gardens; and *Learning For Life: Singapore's Investment in Lifelong Learning Since the 1950s* (2014), about a key brand attribute of Singapore's manpower resource.